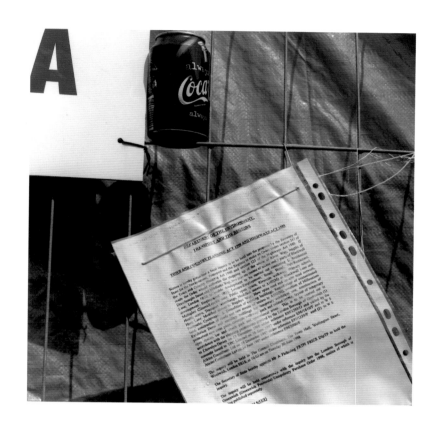

THE MILLENNIUM
DOME

ELIZABETH WILHIDE

Foreword by the Prime Minister,
the Rt Hon TONY BLAIR MP

TED SMART

Contents

Foreword by the Prime Minister, the Rt Hon Tony Blair MP

The millennium is an important time for us all to reflect on our common past, the present we share, and the future we will help to shape. In this country, at this time, I believe we can stand proud as a forward-looking people who are breaking down old-fashioned barriers, building a multiracial Britain that works, seizing new opportunities, creating new products, building strong communities. I am confident that, in the next millennium as in this, the British people will be characterized by their ingenuity, their determination and their compassion.

We will celebrate the millennium with a new dynamism in our country. The Millennium Dome symbolizes this dynamism. It is fittingly sited by the prime meridian at Greenwich – the 'home of time'. Its breathtaking design has captured the imagination throughout the world. Its exhibits will provide a powerful and fascinating presentation of life in the United Kingdom at the end of the second millennium – who we are, what we do, and what the future may have in store for us.

I believe all of us will be proud of the Millennium Experience, and that the year 2000 will be a time we look back on with pride and pleasure. I want it to be remembered as a period when we all came together to celebrate and to make a difference for the future.

Tony Blair

Introduction

The Dome is not a building. It is not even a dome. It has the profile of a shallow dome, but none of its structural properties. It looks something like a tent, but it is not a tent either. In engineering terms it is a cable-net structure, more closely related to a suspension bridge than St Paul's. In the architect's comfortable phrase its fabric roof is a 'loose-fit overcoat', a cover that provides a flexible weatherproof enclosure for what it shelters. It is soft and hard, rounded and spiky; it hugs the ground and reaches for the sky. A simple idea achieved in a complex way, its elegance conceals the depth of analysis required to achieve it. A knitted web, a network, an envelope, its structural tensions make explicit the turning point of time it has been designed to mark.

Throughout its period of conception and construction, the Dome has been one of the most reviled projects ever undertaken in Britain. People who have not seen it, or set foot in it, have happily hated it from a distance. It has died a hundred times over, buried under banner headlines and column inches of press. It has proved the lightning conductor of every pre-millennial tension, the butt of every barroom joke, the chattering classes' *bête noire*. Yet, in another of the Dome's strange paradoxes, such violent antipathies can be blown away in the very first minutes of a visit. The most vocal opponents of the scheme become instant converts; fence-sitters fall off their fences. In the end, the Dome has to be experienced to be believed. It is its own best advocate.

The most obviously impressive aspect of the Dome is its size; it is the largest structure of its kind in the world. But size means more than 'bigger' or 'biggest' – at this scale the superlatives shift from one category into another altogether. The Dome is so big that quantity becomes a different quality. Here, size is in the eye of the beholder. Inside this vast structure, the eye plays tricks, it lies about what it sees, until a human ant or a matchbox truck halfway across the expanse brings a sharp adjustment of scale and an even sharper intake of breath.

'The Dome is a conundrum,' says Mike Davies of Richard Rogers Partnership, who has led the architectural team on site. 'It's a conundrum of scale, space, perspective, form. . . . There are many things about the Dome that you can't understand until you are here.'

For Alex Madina, New Millennium Experience Company content editor, the most striking characteristic of the Dome is its elusive quality: 'People think they've got a handle on it. But I don't think the Dome is a graspable structure. I've been sitting around it, walking through it and climbing up it but there are only brief moments when I have grasped its scale. The Dome is clever in that way. The genius of it is that actually the meaning keeps on eluding you.'

If it is difficult to comprehend the scale of the Dome when you are actually standing inside it, baldly stated on paper, its vital statistics mean even less. Its twelve steel masts are 100 metres high. Over 70 kilometres of high-strength cabling make up the cable-net structure.

The Dome has an overall diameter of 365 metres, an internal diameter of 320 metres, a circumference of a kilometre and is 50 metres high at its central point. It encloses a ground-floor area of over 80,000 square metres. Your feet may tell you what a kilometre feels like to walk around, but what do the other numbers mean? For most of us, the definition of a large building is a tall building; as we scurry past at ground level, we can vaguely sense what looms above us. We know that a fifty-storey building is very high, because we are used to houses with only one, two or three floors. But while the Dome is certainly high enough, its scale has more to do with volume and the vast area it encloses.

Recognizing that many people find such enormities difficult to comprehend without translation, the New Millennium Experience Company has helpfully come up with a series of telling comparisons, 'fun facts', if you like. It may or may not be useful to know how long Niagara Falls would take to fill the Dome, should it ever be turned upside down or, indeed, how much this would represent in terms of pints of beer or Olympic-sized swimming pools (answers: about fifteen minutes; 3.8 billion; and 1,100, respectively). For those who naturally find they measure things in double-deckers, the fact sheet will tell you that 18,000 of them could fit into the Dome. But if you prefer to think in terms of landmarks, rather than volumes of liquid or buses, it may be more instructive to discover that the Dome equals thirteen Albert Halls, ten St Paul's Cathedrals, two Wembley Stadiums, or two Georgia Domes. It is as high as Nelson's Column or the Statue of Liberty (without its base). It encloses an area twice the size of Trafalgar Square covering all the surrounding buildings including Admiralty Arch; it could accommodate the Eiffel Tower lying on its side . . . and the Great Pyramid of Giza comes into it somewhere. What no statistic or fun fact can truly convey, however, is the unique nature of this project and how it has been achieved.

Every building project has its deadlines, but few deadlines loom so large or are quite so immovable as that of the Dome. Only four years ago, the Greenwich peninsula was the largest undeveloped

site in London, a 300-acre expanse of polluted and derelict land scarred by many decades of heavy industrial use. When Greenwich was chosen to stage the millennium celebrations in February 1996, time was short enough. What then ensued was a protracted period of uncertainty. In the succeeding months, while the Dome's planners, consultants and designers worked on against the odds, the future of the entire project still hung in the balance. The scheme was submitted for planning application in October 1996; planning approval was granted at the beginning of 1997, but it was not until June 1997, after the new Labour government came to power, that the project finally had a certain future. The consequence of such delays has been a design and construction programme that might just as effectively be measured in minutes as in months. Time, which informs the theme of the Millennium Experience itself, has been the Dome's greatest obstacle.

Finance has been another. Not a penny of the £758 million budget comes from tax revenue: it does not represent money that would otherwise be spent building hospitals or schools, but comprises a Lottery grant supplemented by sponsorship and commercial income. Despite the scale of this massive budget, the subject of so much heated public controversy, there has, in reality, been no more money to play with than time. The budget must fund not only the Dome and its associated infrastructure, but also its contents – the exhibitions and shows and their associated running costs throughout the year of millennial celebration – as well as contributing to a national programme of activities, many of which have been scheduled to run over two years. In the light of the many long-term aims and objectives of the Millennium Experience – benefits to the Greenwich area and the country as a whole which will last for generations – this sum begins to look much less substantial. The structure of the Dome itself represents an extremely economical solution to the problem of covering such an enormous area, costing about the same to build per square metre as an average out-of-town retail warehouse. The fact that it is a beautifully expressive and inspiring structure, rather than a lowest-common-denominator shed, is witness to the imaginative and visionary powers of its designers.

Given such constraints of time and money, the Dome is a remarkable creative and technical accomplishment. But those working on the project have also imposed their own benchmarks, dedicating themselves to best practice in the fields of environmental design, transport policy and operational efficiency. Often working from first principles and without precedent, architects, engineers and designers have responded to site, context and brief in a highly ambitious way. This is all the more surprising since there is no safety net for failure and next to no tolerance for error: the Dome must run, and run well, from a standing start. It is the architectural and constructional equivalent of a high-wire act.

The breathtaking scale of the Dome is revealed in this sequence of aerial photographs. Clearly visible as a white dot in the centre of the satellite picture *(top)*, it dominates the Greenwich peninsula. Focusing closer in, it is seen at a scale of around 1: 33,000 *(middle)* and, nearer still, of 1: 5,000 *(bottom)*.

THE CRYSTAL PALACE IN HYDE PARK FOR GRAND INTERNATIONAL EXHIBITION 1851

In form, the Dome is deceptively simple. Before the panels of roof fabric were installed, the exposed cable net resembled nothing so much as a spider's web, a basic natural structure with which it shares many engineering principles. But this simplicity has been achieved with the highest levels of technical skill demanding the utmost precision. The largest section of roof fabric weighs more than a tonne, yet an error of just one centimetre in the construction of either the fabric or the cable net that supports it would have meant that roof and structure simply would not have fitted together. From the abseilers who tensioned the cables, to the managers who coordinated the complex lines of communication, building the Dome has been a series of similarly exacting tests – literally the challenge of a lifetime.

Visiting the site as the digital countdown clock ticked off the seconds, you might have expected to find mayhem and more than a little rising panic. Instead, the site was a disciplined, positive environment, with people working at full stretch and seemingly enjoying every minute of it. The atmosphere was quite unlike that of any other major building site or corporate enterprise. The range of talents and expertise working at close quarters, the integration of disciplines and sheer sense of purpose were hugely compelling.

This spirit was all the more surprising when one considers that the Dome came into being amid a constant background hum of disapproval. It is no secret that even before the first pile was driven into the Greenwich site, the Dome had acted as a focus for every conceivable form of contemporary dissatisfaction.

In particular, the Dome has proved a public relations gift for environmental groups, serving as a convenient hook for a variety of well-publicized single-interest campaigns. Misconceptions, consequently, are rife. From the recycling of runoff water from the roof, and

The Great Exhibition of All Nations in 1851 took place in Hyde Park in the immense glass structure of the Crystal Palace. Despite predictable criticism, the exhibition was hugely successful with the general public, as revealed in a contemporary cartoon by George Cruikshank, showing an excited crowd dashing to catch an exhibition-bound bus.

A century after the Great Exhibition, the Festival of Britain in 1951 provided a boost to national morale after the privations of wartime. The thrilling modernity of the Skylon *(top left)* and the Dome of Discovery, shown here under construction *(left)* and finished *(above)*, expressed a new, progressive and forward-looking direction.

the flushing of the toilets, to the greening of the river edge, a high standard of environmental practice runs right the way through the project. In this context, the Dome's role as a catalyst for the regeneration and remediation of the entire peninsula site has been perhaps most important. These works, conceived within the Richard Rogers Partnership's masterplan, and carried out by English Partnerships, the government urban regeneration agency, include walkways, parks, new habitats for native species and riverside development, all designed in accordance with the latest ecological thinking.

Controversy has always been a feature of major enterprises, particularly at a national level: the Great Exhibition of 1851 and the Festival of Britain a century later attracted their fair share. However, this type of response is not unique to Britain. Mike Davies also worked on the Pompidou Centre in Paris and is used to carrying through hugely ambitious schemes in the face of seemingly implacable public and professional opinion: 'Pompidou was a larger project than the Dome in its time – and virtually the same words that were used in the original petition against the Eiffel Tower were being used in the petition sent in to protest against the Pompidou Centre. Virtually identical words. It was ironical that nearly a hundred years had passed between the two.' The Dome has suffered similar invective.

> *The Dome is essentially a big umbrella for our climate. And I hope it's a very beautiful umbrella. It's big because it marks a big moment in time. It's an optimistic statement about the potential of the present and future: it's about how one can better control one's destiny and at the same time enjoy oneself.*
>
> Richard Rogers, Richard Rogers Partnership

The scale, efficiency and economy of the Dome have been achieved using the most advanced levels of technology, in design, engineering and planning. Yet its elemental form recalls much earlier forms of building, from primitive shelters to basic structures in the natural world. 'Once you understand technology very, very well it becomes similar to nature and begins to work with it,' says Gregor Harvie, who, in the

> *We wanted something that was festive in spirit. Although the Dome is not a tent, it has the image of a tent or marquee, an image that is festive; it's to do with celebration; it's to do with 'the circus comes to town'. And it's no accident that those masts reach up at that angle like raised arms, and say 'Yes!'*
>
> Mike Davies, Richard Rogers Partnership

capacity of 'technical troubleshooter', has worked on the project from the beginning. The synthesis of old and new, high and low technology, is what makes the Dome, poised at this turning point in time, such a fitting symbol of where we have been and where we might go.

Getting in the festive spirit – like the Skylon, the soaring masts of the Dome are powerful markers of celebration. Both also share the same 'cigar' shaped profile, revealing their engineering similarities.

Context

The Dome has a powerful and memorable form. For political cartoonists, the image has proved infinitely adaptable: the Dome is Michael Heseltine's hairstyle, Tony Blair's grin, William Hague's bald pate; turned upside down, it's a fruitbowl for the Banana War; in the opening credits of a topical television news quiz it is punctured by a fusillade of satirical darts. Somehow it has managed to get under everyone's skin. Research conducted before a single penny had been spent promoting and marketing the Millennium Experience revealed that the Dome had a 'penetration factor' of 92 per cent.

The simple 'rightness' of the Dome's design has an air of inevitability about it. It appears to be the way it is simply because it is the way it is. But the story of how the Dome came to be conceived reveals no such inevitability.

All projects of this size and national importance attract attention. Most, however, start with some fixed points – at the very least a client, a site and an identifiable need or purpose. The Dome is different. Its origins were little more than the desire to mark a momentous calendrical change in some significant way. There was no site, and the precise extent and nature of the funding was not known. There was no company to run the project or to act as the client. There was no brief, beyond a wish list of aspirations.

Nothing like the Dome has ever existed before, certainly not on such a scale. Neither are there precedents within living memory for marking a millennium. The result has been that the Dome's design has developed within the context of an evolving brief and a changing organizational structure. Creating the entire millennium project has often meant creating entirely new ways of doing things.

No one is more aware of this than Jennie Page who, as former chief executive of the Millennium Commission and now chief executive of the New Millennium Experience Company, has been involved with the project since its beginnings: 'The structure expresses what the project itself is, which is a great overarching complicated knitted web holding down something vast and semi-opaque.'

In a simple sense, the whole notion of time has informed both the brief of the Dome and the selection of its site on the meridian line at Greenwich. The millennium, as a deadline, has proved a powerful creative force, serving to concentrate the mind wonderfully. In design terms, however, the impact of 'time' has been the Dome's built-in flexibility. 'An engineering response to indecision', is how Ian Liddell, who has led the Dome's engineering team, rather wryly puts it. The Dome was conceived both as a way of keeping options open, while these options were still being defined, and as a way of ensuring that the designers of what it would contain – the Millennium Experience – had maximum time to develop and realize their own ideas. In this sense, the form of the Dome anticipated its function, its 'loose fit' representing a supremely practical response to 'open-endedness'. It served, above all, to create a flexible space with the potential to be used in many different ways, an inbuilt quality that in years to come will prove one of its greatest assets.

The Dome is a tensioned structure, where enormous energies pull and tug against each other. It is no accident that it is the product of equally strong creative tensions. But the resolution of these tensions in the design process has rarely been achieved in single eureka-style moments of blinding clarity. The pattern, and it is a pattern that has run the whole way through the project, has been one of constant fluidity and redefinition, a cumulative shift of endless possibilities towards a final goal.

The taut, white roof of the Dome comprises fabric panels only 1mm thick. Tensioned between the cable-net structure, this minimal covering can withstand enormous loads.

Prehistory

What is the significance of a change of millennium? How should it be marked or celebrated? Where should such celebrations take place? Who should create them? Who should run them? How should they be paid for? In the early 1990s, such fundamental questions were just beginning to be asked. The way in which these questions have subsequently been answered has provided the context for the Dome. It has been a rather public and politically charged way of formulating a brief.

Like Christmas, which always seems a long way off until it is suddenly round the corner, it has taken psychological time to square off and face the millennium. It was 1992 before the idea of marking the millennium first appeared on a political wish list, when it turned up in the pages of the Conservative Party's election manifesto. The idea for making the 'millennium' one of the beneficiaries of the National Lottery is said to have come from the then Prime Minister, John Major.

National celebrations, festivals or monuments cost money. There is good reason to suspect that the idea of a millennial celebration and the idea of a National Lottery were not entirely independent in conception. The Conservative government was committed to low taxation and tight controls on public spending. With no money likely to be forthcoming from tax revenue and the end of the century fast approaching, the launch of the Lottery was certainly timely, as Jennie Page acknowledges: 'It's all fortuitous. If there hadn't been new money, we wouldn't be doing anything like this.' Had the Lottery not existed, someone would have had to have invented it.

New money, new ways of spending it. After the National Lottery Act was passed in 1993, the Millennium Commission was set up to act as a distributor of lottery funds, awarding grant money to projects that would in some way mark the millennium. Unlike other Lottery distributors – such as the Arts and Sports councils – the Millennium Commission was always going to have a relatively short active life. More to the point, as yet it had no defined purpose. 'Quite clearly no one had actually thought about a millennium before,' says Jennie Page.

The government's response to these unknowns was to create an organization with strong political representation. The new Commission comprised two Ministers of the Crown, together with an Opposition nominee, and six independents, brought in to represent radically different areas of life. The first chair was the Rt Hon Peter Brooke, CH, MP, Secretary of State for National Heritage (now renamed as the Department of Culture, Media and Sport). This appointment set a precedent; ever since, it has been customary for the secretary of state to be the chair of the Commission.

After preliminary consultations and a nationwide exercise in opinion-gathering, in June 1994 the Commission announced that it proposed to spend the money it expected to receive from the Lottery in three ways: on capital projects, awards to individuals, and to fund a festival or festivities to mark the year 2000. As Jennie Page explains, the special nature of the millennium as a unique event posed certain fundamental difficulties when it came to the last funding category: 'The underlying problem was that while it was perfectly easy to get people to apply competitively for money to do all sorts of different millennium projects around the country – capital projects – and you could construct a sensible competitive basis on which the Commission could exercise judgement between various bids for money or grants, it's very difficult to make that system work when you're talking about a unique event. There's no pre-existing market, as it were, in people who run exhibitions once every thousand years.'

Like the other Lottery distributors, the Millennium Commission cannot run anything itself, but can only invite and respond to grant applications. Some parameters, however, had to be put in place. While it was agreed that those who would be putting forward proposals for the festival should be allowed to express their own views, it was also acknowledged that it was unfair to expect such proposals to come out of a vacuum. First it was decided to hold the festival at a single site, to give a focus to the celebrations. The next step was to identify potential sites which could satisfy what had emerged as the Commission's base requirements for the festival: that it should have the capacity for at least 10 million visitors; that it should run for a year; that at least half the visits could be achieved by public transport; and that there was the capacity to leave a legacy. With Arup Associates acting as consultants, dossiers of information were prepared on all the potential sites around the country which met these criteria. A competition was held and four preferred sites emerged: Birmingham National Exhibition Centre (NEC); the Derby 'Pride' site next to the railway station; Stratford in east London; and the Greenwich peninsula. These final four were announced in July 1995 by Virginia Bottomley, who had succeeded Peter Brooke as Heritage Secretary and chair of the Commission.

Having identified the sites in the running, in August 1995 the Commission held a conference at the QE2 Conference Centre to set

Sited opposite Canary Wharf, the Dome represents a shift in London's centre of gravity towards the east, an area in sore need of economic regeneration.

out its stall and drum up interest in the project as a whole. At that time, it was envisaged that the Commission would be making up to £250 million of Lottery funds available for the festival. The purpose of the conference was to demonstrate the potential of a national exhibition, and outline the long-term legacy and commercial development that was expected to follow on from such a high-profile event.

What then followed was a two-stage 'invitation-to-tender' process. There were fifteen responses to the first request for outline proposals, of which four were short-listed. 'Of course what you get is the absolutely barking mad at the first stage as well as the perfectly sane,' says Jennie Page. The four proposals on the short list came from consortia that appeared to have sufficient backing, land interest or potential to be worth a second look. When these four were invited to work up their proposals in greater detail in the autumn of 1995, one withdrew because it was party to a take-over bid, and two of the remaining three 'fell into each other's arms' and combined efforts. That left two proposals in the running. The first was from what Jennie Page describes as the 'unholy marriage' and had 'more people associated with it than pages in its proposal'. The other proposal left, an 'extraordinarily well-worked-up and inspirational scheme', came from the design group Imagination Limited, working in association with the management of Birmingham's NEC.

Imagination (and its director Gary Withers) had a long history of involvement with the NEC, going back some twenty years; the firm was extremely experienced in the production of large world-class shows. Imagination's partner, the NEC, was no less familiar on the exhibition circuit. In its capacity as an international conference and trade fair centre, the NEC was a favoured location for many commercial companies and had immense operational experience. But as one of the sites identified by the Commission as suitable for a millennium exhibition, the NEC had other persuasive advantages. Located in the centre of Britain, it was relatively easier for more people to reach than London within the notional journey time of two and a half hours. It was a flat, serviced site, by far the least problematic.

Nevertheless, the Greenwich peninsula site was still very much in contention, thanks in part to some vigorous lobbying by Greenwich Council and its local partners, as well as other interested parties. Michael Heseltine, then one of the government's representatives on the Millennium Commission, had made it clear that in his view, if Lottery money was going to spent, it should help regenerate a brownfield site somewhere in the city, while the *Evening Standard* was mounting a particularly vocal pro-London campaign. Greenwich was, however, infinitely further back than Birmingham in terms of development. The site was owned by British Gas, who were not looking to be full partners in a new scheme. The extension to the Jubilee Line was planned, but a long way from delivery. The site was deeply contaminated and virtually derelict.

In the early part of January 1996, the Commission announced that neither of the two detailed bids that it had received was strictly compliant with the brief, although they remained very taken with Imagination's proposals. Imagination had indicated in its original bid that they were prepared to offer an exhibition on a site other than Birmingham. The Commission decided to ask Imagination to work up a 'Greenwich version' to the same level as their Birmingham proposal so that a choice could be made between the two.

If Greenwich had conspicuous disadvantages, viewed the other way round these could equally be seen as significant recommendations for its selection. One of the key criteria for the millennium exhibition was that it should leave a 'legacy'. The Greenwich peninsula, a site that had been lying empty for twenty years, in a depressed urban area that desperately needed an economic kick-start, offered legacy potential in spades. World fairs and expos in the past have often been used to achieve such aims: the regeneration of Barcelonetta, in the run-down harbour area of Barcelona, is a recent case in point. But beyond such practical, tangible, down-to-earth aspirations, there was something else about the Greenwich site that had an even more insistent pull. As the 'home of world time', with the meridian line actually passing through the peninsula, the symbolic parallels were too strong to ignore. As Jennie Page explains, 'It was the combination of the sense that there was something deeply consonant between what we were marking and the site, together with the economic and social regeneration potential, which made people keen.'

In February 1996, the Millennium Commission announced that Greenwich would be the millennial site. The choice had been made, and it was far from the easy option.

Greenwich

Greenwich Council and its local partners had actively campaigned for over three years to have the borough recognized as the geographical focus for the millennium celebrations. As the 'home of world time', the appropriateness of Greenwich was clear enough. But local campaigners had other compelling reasons. The area, while rich in historical association, had high levels of unemployment and deprivation. Between 1991 and 1993 some 500 businesses and 10,000 jobs were lost in Greenwich, the largest reduction in any London borough; the gasworks on the peninsula site alone once employed 3,000. One in three of all unemployed people in London live in the surrounding Thames Gateway boroughs, reflecting the area's economic decline as docks closed and heavy industry departed from the city. Transport infrastructure was

The prime meridian, or zero degrees longitude, bisects the Royal Observatory at Greenwich, founded in the late 1670s. The prime meridian is where the third millennium officially begins.

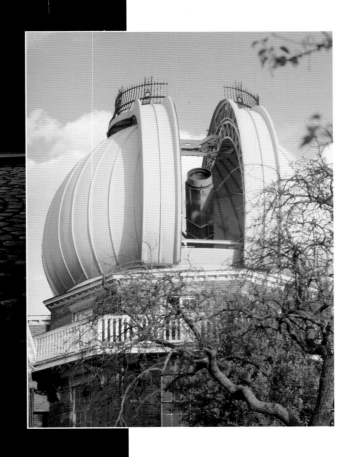

Greenwich, in southeast London, is an area rich in historical and maritime associations. A photograph taken in 1856 shows Greenwich Park in the foreground, overlooked by the Queen's House, designed by Inigo Jones *(left)*. The domes of the Royal Naval College, situated on the river, rise up behind. A newcomer to the Greenwich skyline, the Dome occupies a former industrial site to the east of the borough *(above)*.

poor, with the Thames, which in centuries past had bustled with river traffic, now no more than an empty highway. Choosing Greenwich as the millennium site offered the chance to open up the river once again and bring the city's prosperity eastwards to kick-start a post-industrial regeneration. It also provided the chance to eradicate the decay and dereliction left by an industrial past.

The economic blight of recent decades, with all its attendant social and environmental stresses, has tended to cast a shadow over Greenwich's more illustrious past, a heritage that is evident in the fine historical buildings grouped around a pretty Georgian town centre and the green swath of Greenwich Park. In centuries past, Greenwich was one of London's outlying pleasure zones, connected to the city by the vital artery of the River Thames. Originally a Celtic fishing village and subsequently a Roman resort, Greenwich was later favoured by successive generations of English monarchs who hunted in its park and built their palaces beside the river. Henry VIII, Mary I and Elizabeth I were all born at Greenwich Palace – or 'Placentia' (the 'pleasant place') – a favourite Tudor residence. It was here that Sir Walter Raleigh chivalrously laid his cloak over a puddle so that Queen Elizabeth I would not get her feet wet.

Greenwich was equally favoured by the Stuarts. The Queen's House, designed by Inigo Jones, originally for James I's wife, Anne of Denmark, was finally completed in 1635 for Queen Henrietta Maria, wife of Charles I. After the Restoration, Charles II commissioned André Le Nôtre, Louis XIV's celebrated landscape designer, to replan Greenwich Park, while Sir Christopher Wren was engaged to design the Royal Observatory in the late 1670s at the top of Greenwich Hill, along with the house of the first Astronomer Royal, John Flamsteed.

Another key Greenwich landmark is the Royal Naval College, formerly the Royal Naval Hospital, built on the site of the old Greenwich Palace. The college consists of four buildings, the earliest of which was originally built as a part of an uncompleted palace for Charles II. The remaining blocks were designed by Wren, assisted by Nicholas Hawksmoor; and Wren's successor, Sir John Vanbrugh, the architect of Blenheim Palace. Lord Nelson lay in state in the Hall of the Naval College in 1805 after his death at the Battle of Trafalgar.

It is Greenwich's maritime connections and, by extension, its significance as the 'home of time' that gives it particular resonance as the site for the millennium celebrations. Flamsteed, the first Astronomer Royal, was not simply employed as an idle gazer into the heavens, but was charged with the important task of calculating and measuring the

> *Greenwich is characterized by a unique combination of decay and opportunity.*
>
> Once in a Thousand Years – A Discussion Paper, Greenwich Waterfront Development Partnership, August 1996

positions of certain stars in relation to the moon; his task was to try to find an astronomical way of determining longitude.

To make astronomical observations, it is necessary to set a meridian, an imaginary – and indeed arbitrary – line from north to south from which measurements can be taken. Since ancient times, astronomers had known how to calculate latitude according to the position of the sun or the Pole Star. Longitude was a different story; centuries of struggle went into the problem. Every fifteen degrees of longitude represents an hour of time. If navigators could work out the time difference between where they were and a known meridian, it would be possible to work out their exact position. This was not so difficult while they were still in sight of land, but at sea it was a different matter. As trade routes spread throughout the globe and explorers set out to chart the unknown, the need for a precise method of measurement became ever more acute, with the rising death toll at sea, as ships lost their way and foundered, acting as a constant reminder of the pressing need for a solution.

One idea was to determine longitude astronomically, and this was the specific reason for the foundation of the Royal Observatory. Nearly a century after its founding, the first Nautical Almanac was published, comprising lunar-distance tables based on the Greenwich meridian. Britain's pre-eminence as a trading nation meant that the Almanac was widely adopted throughout the world. But in the eighteenth century, the longitude solution finally came from a surprising quarter. After more than forty years devoted to the problem, John Harrison, a clockmaker, came up with a mechanical answer: an instrument that could keep perfect time at sea, or as it is now known, the chronometer. A red ball, dropped down a pole at the top of the Royal Observatory each day at precisely 1pm, became the signal for ships to set their chronometers accurately before setting sail.

Until the nineteenth century every country tended to choose its own capital as a meridian or the fixed point for zero degrees longitude; the United States alone had over 300 time zones. With the advent of the railways and increased commercialization and communication, such localized time systems became increasingly unworkable. The emergence of a transport infrastructure, connecting towns in hours rather than days, brought the need for radical simplification. When one considers the implications of drawing up a railway timetable when there were innumerable time differences across a region – four minutes between Oxford and London, to cite just one example – it is obvious how urgently that standard was required.

The Dome's peninsula site was once home to one of the largest gasworks in Europe, as these photographs taken at the beginning of the 1950s reveal *(above and above right)*. After the departure of heavy industry and the closure of the docks, east London has seen successive attempts at economic regeneration. A photograph taken in 1976 *(right)* shows the area prior to the development of Docklands, with the peninsula in the centre right of the view.

In 1852, Britain adopted 'London time', or Greenwich Mean Time (GMT); in 1883, GMT was also adopted by the United States. At an International Conference in Washington in 1884 it was finally agreed that the meridian passing through Greenwich should be adopted as the prime meridian of the world, dividing East from West. The vote was 22–1, with only San Domingo voting against. As most mariners were already effectively using charts based on the Greenwich meridian, it was a decision rooted in practicality more than anything else. Adopting the Greenwich meridian as the prime meridian had another important consequence: it set the beginning of the 'universal day for all purposes'. The universal day would 'begin for all the world at the moment of mean midnight of the initial meridian', the meridian being defined as the line that passes through the centre of the 'Transit Circle' telescope at the Royal Observatory.

The prime meridian, or zero degrees longitude, is where the third millennium officially begins.

The site

The choice of the Greenwich peninsula as the millennium site may have had significance but it also had profound practical implications for the development of the project. In the first instance, it served to enhance what were already considerable logistical difficulties. The site was, to say the least, a challenging one in almost every respect. Derelict, polluted and with little existing infrastructure, it brought both enormous potential for regeneration together with a new layer of practical difficulties to the task ahead.

The millennium site is situated at the northeastern end of the peninsula, bordered on three sides by the River Thames, between Bugsby's Reach and Blackwall Reach. A former coaling pier – a visible feature of the opening credits of the long-running soap *Eastenders* – occupies the eastern riverside edge of the site. Open and exposed to the weather, conditions on the peninsula can be bleak and downright inhospitable in the depths of winter or when the wind blows from the wrong direction – there is said to be no land higher than 100 metres between the site and the steppes of Russia.

One of the largest undeveloped areas in London, the peninsula had a recent history of heavy industrial use. The largest gasworks in Europe once occupied part of the site, together with a tar works and a benzene works; for twenty years and more, after industrial activity ceased, the land had been left derelict. The portion of the gasworks that had occupied the site had been devoted to gas 'scrubbing' and purification. Scrubbing consisted of removing ammonia from the gas with water; purification consisted of passing the gas through crushed chalk or lime to remove hydrogen sulphide and other unpleasant chemicals. As would

eventually be discovered, the residue of this latter process – the 'spent' or 'foul' lime – had simply been dumped on the ground, up to four metres deep in places. Other pollutants included tar from the tar works and BTEX (benzene, toluene ethyl-benzene and xylene) from the benzene works. British Gas, the owners of the land at the time the site was selected, were engaged in statutory remediation – a basic cleanup – prior to its sale, but significant pollutants remained in the ground. Moreover, the site was not fully cleared of structures, some of which had buried foundations. Ground conditions were also uncertain, although the site's former name before industrialization, 'Bugsby's Marsh', provided an indication of what these might be.

A particularly significant underground feature of the site is the southbound carriageway of the Blackwall Tunnel, which crosses from the north side of the river and emerges at ground level in the northern part of the peninsula, northwest of the site. This meant that loading would be restricted directly over the tunnel and that any construction taking place within 67 metres of it would have to be specially approved by the Highways Agency. Within the site itself is a large concrete structure that is the air vent for the tunnel. This ventilation shaft is surrounded by a ring of land that is dedicated to the Highways Agency for tunnel access.

This, then, was the basic raw material with which the designers had to work. Exposed, polluted, with a tunnel running under it, a large ventilation shaft in the middle of it, and with the likelihood of soft ground conditions, the physical limitations of the millennium site could not have been more severe.

The Greenwich masterplan

The Greenwich peninsula, as the millennium site, may have been derelict, but in terms of design it was not precisely a blank sheet. An important consequence of Greenwich's selection was that the project inherited the expertise of Richard Rogers Partnership, the world-famous architectural practice, who were working on a masterplan of the entire peninsula site. This masterplan was being prepared for English Partnerships, the government urban regeneration agency, who were in the process of buying the land from British Gas.

The architects' specific mandate was to design an infrastructure for the peninsula, including main roads, and to come up with a mixed-use development strategy that integrated the proposals within the existing Greenwich environment. It was a rare opportunity. Sites in cities like London are generally driven by road pattern, or they are opportunistic patches that can only be infilled in certain ways. The peninsula offered the chance to think afresh about larger issues, such as orientation to sun and wind, ecology and the treatment of the river edge.

The development site as a whole occupied 300 acres; the portion to be dedicated to the millennium exhibition, at the northeastern end, was 181 acres, just over half the total area. The arrangement was that the millennium site would be leased from English Partnerships for the proposed year of the exhibition, after which time the site would revert to their ownership. This arrangement immediately brought local 'legacy' issues into play as far as the design process was concerned.

As it emerged, there were to be huge areas of commonality between the masterplan proposals and the Dome. Richard Rogers Partnership envisaged a spine of green running up the middle of the peninsula, linking open areas, which would enable people to walk or cycle from one end of the peninsula to the other. Larger blocks of building were planned for the northeastern side, the side most exposed to wind, to act as a shelter – or 'shoulders and overcoats' for the rest of the site. The mile-long green armature, starting with a southern green space, continuing in a central park and finishing with a meadow area near the river, was an important unifier for the whole peninsula, but served to create more local spaces as well.

The end of this rounded peninsula had always suggested some form of circular infrastructure, and basic road layouts that followed the lay of the land. When Greenwich won the bid for the millennium celebrations, it was natural to pair the existing design work with the new proposals. Richard Rogers Partnership was given the specific mandate to coordinate with Imagination (and their engineering consultants Buro Happold) on the infrastructure of the exhibition in such a way that as much legacy as possible could be 'levered' out of the project: in other words to find ways in which short-term objectives and long-term priorities could coincide. From the start, it was a synergistic combination.

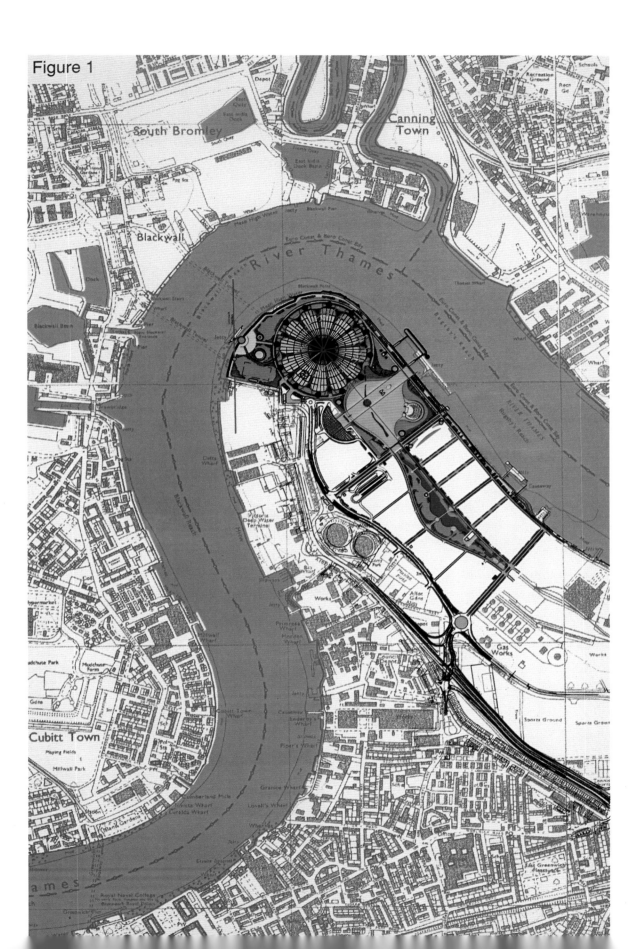

Figure 1

The masterplan for the regeneration of the Greenwich peninsula has been prepared by Richard Rogers Partnership for the government urban regeneration agency, English Partnerships *(far left)*. The map of the masterplan, after the conception of the Dome, shows the areas of commonality between the millennium site and the long-term plans for the peninsula as a whole *(left)*.

The birth of the Dome

The Dome has been created by teamwork. In part, this is a function of its scale, as Jennie Page acknowledges: 'The only way you get big things done is by using lots and lots and lots of people.' Mike Davies agrees: 'Gone are the days of Frank Lloyd Wright doing an individual house and stamping around and rowing with the contractor and throwing his ego about and winning or losing as the case may be. The scale of these projects is such that they cannot be achieved by one person or one small group. It has to be enormously complex teamwork. You count on each other.' But teamwork, at this level, also has a dynamic quality which is the product of competing creative forces. Peter Rice, in his book *An Engineer Imagines*, makes an important distinction between the positive and negative senses of the term:

'Teamwork is a much misused word, often used as a cover for blandness, or as a salute to others by someone claiming the credit and identity for some important artefact. Good teams are made up of different people, people whose separateness and attitude complement each other, and who by their individual willingness to work together and accept the presence and contribution of all the others, for a while at least, make possible real momentum.'

The Dome is considered by all who have been involved to be the product of a group of people — architect, engineer, construction team and client — working to a shared philosophy. Mike Davies, of Richard Rogers Partnership, has first-hand experience of the value of the team approach. Renowned for such landmark projects as the Pompidou Centre in Paris and the Lloyd's Building in London, Richard Rogers Partnership has a working culture that is entirely based on dynamic teamwork, both within the office and with its associated consultants.

'The art of any great project is to build the right team, more than anything else — a team which is spiritually on song with each other,' says

> *We're more engineering-sympathetic than most people and our architecture shows it. Our architecture is informed by engineering as much as anything else. I don't believe that architecture and engineering should really be separable. Where architecture stops and engineering begins on this project you really can't say. It was absolutely conceptually locked in from the beginning.*
>
> Mike Davies, Richard Rogers Partnership

Mike Davies. 'If you are aware as an engineer that you are at the front end of your profession it gives you a different attitude than if you think you are run-of-the-mill. The same is true in architecture. You've got to have someone who's strong enough to dialogue with you, engineers with enough guts and confidence to say, "I disagree with you, Mr or Miss Architect", and similarly the other way round. Give me a talented person that I'm going to have a difficult time with, rather than a non-talented person that I can tell what to do, any time. You feed off their talent, they feed off your talent and the solution that's derived has its qualities in the integrity of all the parties involved.'

At the heart of the Dome's design process was the creative relationship that evolved between the architects and the engineers. Engineers, traditionally viewed as the back-room boys and girls of the design world, have never quite shaken off an unwarranted reputation for dullness. In the public mind, engineers are perceived as the full stops, the fail-safes, answering a firmly structural 'because' to the architect's 'why not?' The worst engineering does takes such caution to extremes, specifying a structural design that, while safe and workable, encumbers creativity with feet of clay. The best engineering, on the other hand, is in itself profoundly creative, innovative and forward-looking; it is the practical application of the technological cutting edge. In the words of Peter Rice: 'The architect's response is primarily creative, whereas the engineer's is essentially inventive.'

Ian Liddell, senior partner of Buro Happold, has led the engineering design team on the Dome. Buro Happold, founded by the late Ted Happold in 1976, is a company that has always been interested in cable and fabric structures, lightweight buildings that make economical and evocative use of the minimum of materials. In 1968 Ted Happold had met Frei Otto, the great German engineer responsible for some memorably innovative structures, such as the West German pavilion at Montreal's Expo 67. The lifelong friendship and collaboration between these two men resulted in a number of other projects that have advanced fabric and cable technology. The firm, whose headquarters are in Bath, is now internationally renowned. With engineering credits as diverse as the National Centre for Popular Music in Sheffield (designed

Creative teamwork: Mike Davies of Richard Rogers Partnership, dressed characteristically in red *(far left)* and Ian Liddell, senior partner of engineering firm Buro Happold *(left)* have led the design teams on the Dome.

by Branson Coates, architects of the Body zone), to the NatWest Media Centre at Lord's Cricket Ground (designed by Future Systems), Buro Happold are well acquainted with the creative tensions implicit in teamwork at the highest level.

The Dome, which has paired a visionary architectural practice with an equally visionary firm of engineers, can be seen either as a highly engineered piece of architecture or as a highly architectural piece of engineering; either way, it represents a new interweaving of disciplines, an approach likely to become increasingly relevant in the future.

Concept

The original Imagination proposal for the Birmingham site consisted of an avenue of pavilions, bolted on, as it were, to the NEC, and making use of all the NEC's facilities. In January 1996 they were asked to look at the potential of putting on the exhibition at Greenwich. As Ian Liddell recalls:

> *The Dome is a true collaboration between architect and engineer. It's one of the few projects where you can't say that either has led. They've both been leading, in a way, each tugging in a different direction. You have the tension between the artistic and the technical which actually does provoke something better from both sides.*
>
> Glyn Trippick, Buro Happold

'Richard Rogers Partnership was developing the masterplan for the whole area. That had a circular road pattern at the end of the peninsula reflecting the shape of the river's edge. Coincidentally, at the same time, Imagination's proposals also had a circular plan. Combining the two designs provided an infrastructure that had a legacy potential.'

Imagination had planned to have twelve main pavilions on the site grouped around a circular arena. Arranged around the pavilions were twelve small spherical structures that would tour the country – the Circle of Time – Gary Wither's imaginative interpretation of an outreach programme. The idea was that, while on tour, they would stimulate different events and activities, before being transported down to Greenwich, where they would come to rest at the millennium exhibition site. 'Gary certainly made a very strong impact in his original proposals for the scope of the exhibition,' says Ian Liddell. 'The National Programme that he was envisaging was really wild, with spheres that toured the country. They were meant to tour from town to town, so you would have this shiny object arriving in the town and staying for a month or two and creating a programme of events around it.'

In the spring of 1996 it was becoming clear that these proposals were going to cost too much. The buildings themselves represented a relatively small amount of the total budget, but the entire concept, with its proposals for their interiors and the National Programme, pushed the costs up too far and the whole budget was rejected. It was back to square one, time to stand back and consider an alternative solution.

Certain other problems had also become apparent rather quickly. 'I'd been to the site and one or two things had struck me about it,' says Mike Davies. 'It was an April day and it was bitterly cold.' The site was very exposed and therefore the need for shelter was fundamental, not merely within the exhibition areas but as people moved about between them. Moreover, there was the fact that the exhibition, unlike other world fairs and expositions which generally run only in the clement months, was due to open in the dead of a British winter and continue throughout the year. Rain – much less freezing winter temperatures – could not be allowed to stop play.

By this point, the programme was looking increasingly tight: there were only three years left, there was an unremediated site, no planning permissions in place and no detailed ideas about what the actual content of the exhibitions would be. It was essential that whatever design solution eventually emerged, it had to save time. The pavilion concept inevitably tied the designers to knowing what would be going on inside each individual exhibition space or building; it was dependent on having a brief for the content or interior before that brief had even had a chance to be developed. What was going to be inside the buildings? How big would the buildings be? Would they all be the same size? What shape would they be? 'In other words, you would have ended up making the mistake of making the brief for the exhibitions fit the buildings,' says Mike Davies.

Traditionally, stand-alone 'expo' buildings, which is what the pavilions would represent, cost at least £1,500 per square metre. The pavilion option would not be cheap. With the pressing issues of time and money, and the problems of the brief, rather than go through twelve individual building processes for each pavilion, it was decided to put one roof over the site and make all the buildings interior exhibits.

'Gary always had the view that it was a nasty cold site and was always complaining about it,' says Ian Liddell. 'He was working on filling in the spaces between the buildings or covering the spaces between the buildings. It was a fairly simple jump to go from that to putting up the cover first and then the buildings underneath.'

At a stroke, the new concept solved certain fundamental difficulties. Firstly, it saved a huge amount of time on the programme. Instead of a series of buildings, only one cover or roof had to be built and that could be constructed quite quickly. Furthermore, the concept allowed a separation to take place between the basic structure and the exhibition

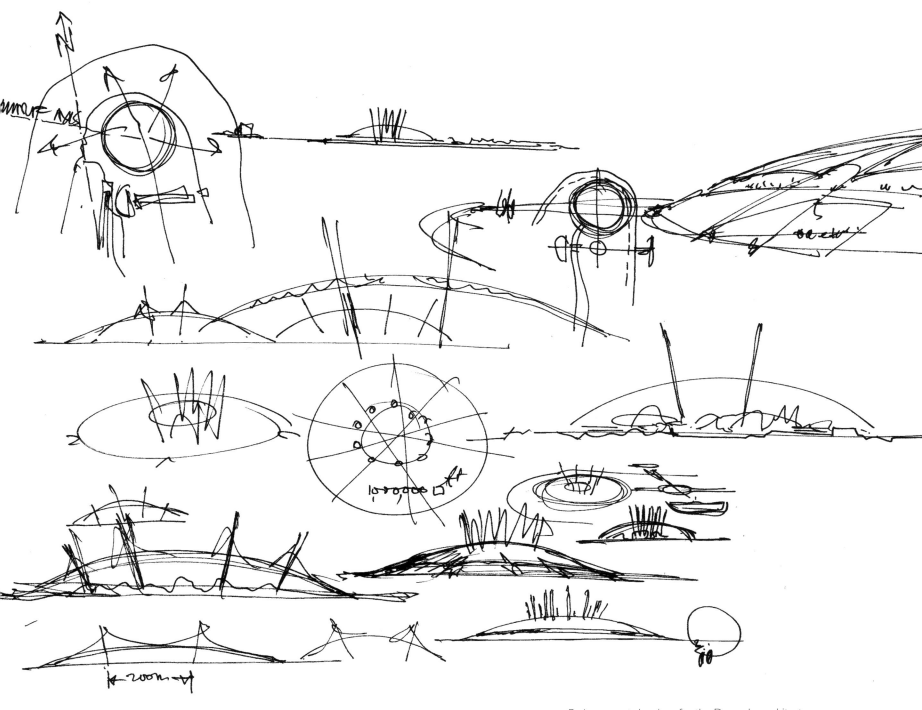

Early concept drawings for the Dome, by architect Mike Davies, dating from May 1996. These sketches show how the Dome's circular outline is a response to the shape of the peninsula and the early stages of its development into a three-dimensional form.

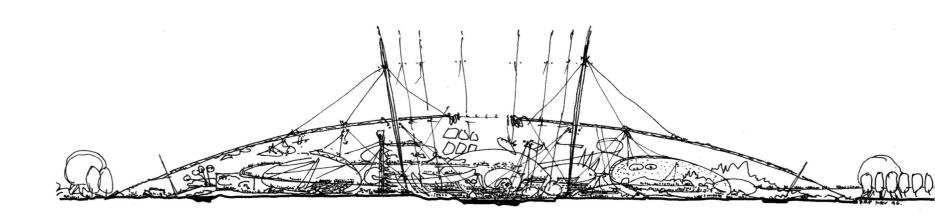

The development of an idea –
Dome sketches by Mike Davies,
dating from early summer 1996.
The Dome has a powerful and
memorable form, which derives
from the essential simplicity of the
concept. Subsequent refinements
occurred during ongoing discussions
between architect and engineer.

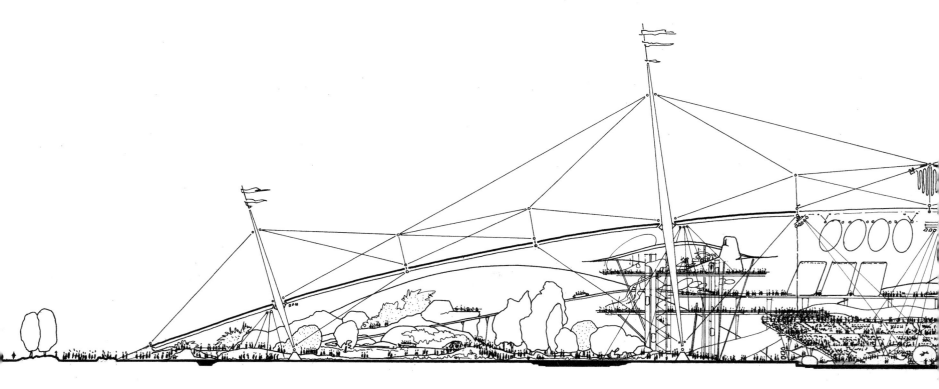

design, without either one compromising the other. It bought time to work out precisely what would be shown inside. The cover, or 'envelope', was very inexpensive, roughly a third of the price that the pavilions would have cost as exhibition buildings; while the pavilions themselves, sheltering under the canopy of the Dome, would also cost less since they would no longer have to be weather-tight. The idea also addressed the physical nature of the site, with its poor ground conditions, which were largely landfill and marsh. At this stage, before site investigations, it was hoped that the new structure could be built with relatively few foundations.

'More importantly,' adds Mike Davies, 'we had to have something that was responding to the scale of the site. It's a unique site. There's no other site in London with water on three sides – it's an absolutely incredible opportunity. Gary had already set the generic interpretation of the north end of the peninsula with the footprint of separate buildings organized in a circle, and that was a sound response. In fact, if you put any kind of rectangle of the massive scale required on the north end of the peninsula it's incredibly uncomfortable. And if you built a big shed, you would hardly notice it from the other side of the river, because that's what everything else is down here – big sheds. You wanted something that was grander in scale and had more identity.'

The concept sketch for the Dome, drawn by Mike Davies, is dated 22 May 1996. It is in red pen, which as anyone who has met the architect will tell you is not surprising: red is clearly his favourite or at least his signature colour, and he is well known for always dressing from head to foot in it. Mike Davies, however, takes pains not to be 'over-credited' as the Dome's designer: 'I have to say that the concept sketch is not that important. The concept sketch helps you start, but dozens of us here are capable of doing the concept sketch. The key thing is then how you hold on to the concept sketch, nurture it and develop it into a design. In that sense, this is very much a team and an office process. The reality is that the firm is the architect of the project. Every act on this project is the result of the whole office worrying about it.'

Once the idea of the Dome had been conceived, Mike Davies and Gary Withers wasted no time bringing in the other half of the design equation – the engineers Buro Happold, particularly Ian Liddell and senior designer Paul Westbury – who had been working with Imagination on their earlier proposals, both at Birmingham and Greenwich. Ian Liddell remembers: 'I got a telephone call from Gary who was sitting talking to Mike Davies and he said, "We're going to cover the site." Then he put me onto Mike, who explained a little bit more about it. So I said, "Fine, we'll do a cable and fabric structure for you," which I did over the weekend, I think it was a Friday, actually. On Monday I said, "How about doing this?" It had a set of masts near the middle and another set of masts out the back. It was 400 metres in diameter because I didn't think that 300 metres would be enough for Gary.'

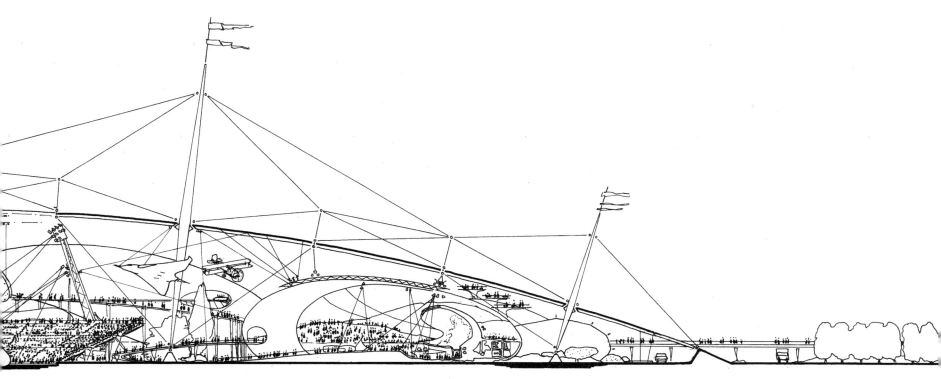

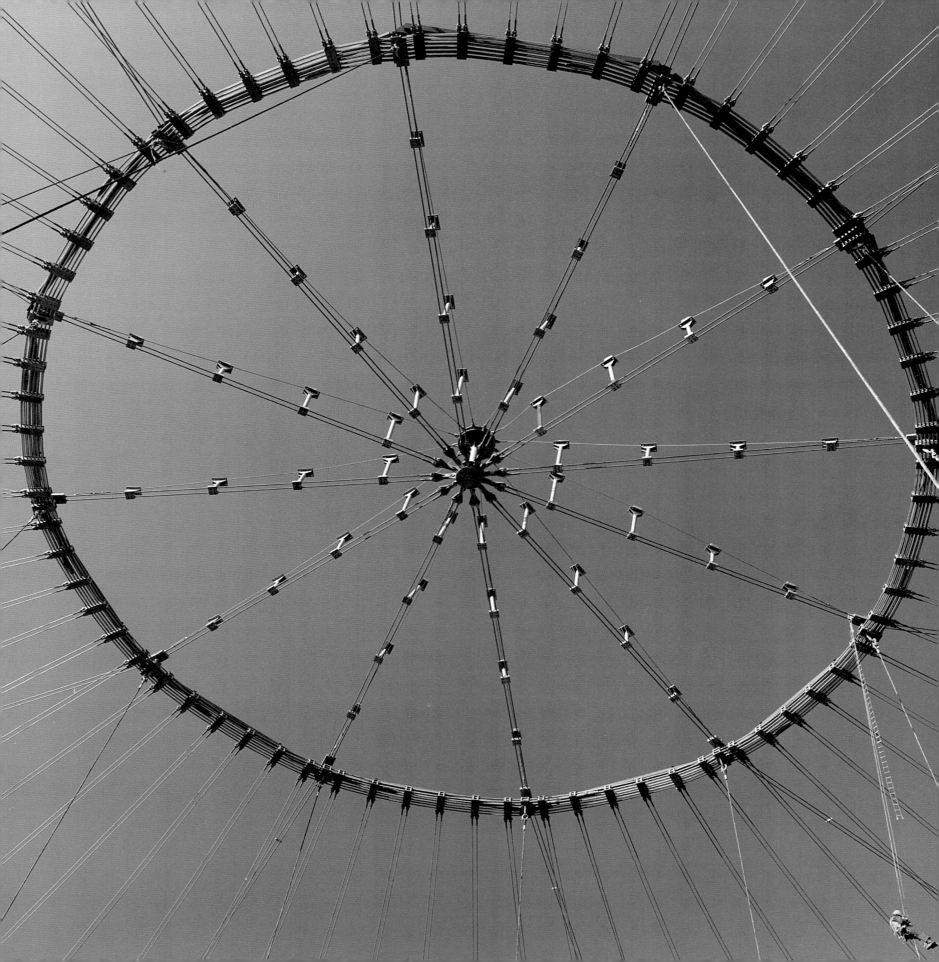

The elegant minimalism of the cable-net structure of the Dome represents a highly efficient use of materials. In engineering terms, it has many similarities to a spider's web. Like the orb web of a common garden spider, the Dome has long lines of radials spanning the distance from centre to perimeter.

Basic principles

The basic engineering concept of the Dome is very simple: stretching cables in tension against cables in tension. Structures based on tension are the reverse of structures based on compression, the latter being the type of structures with which most people are familiar; where tension is pull, compression is push. As Glyn Trippick, partner of Buro Happold, explains: 'The Dome is not an upside-down saucer that sits on the ground. It's actually pulling out of the ground.' In other words, structurally speaking, the Dome is not a dome at all.

In cable-net structures, grids or nets formed of cables stretched at right angles to each other can be given different shapes, depending on the patterning of the grid, how the boundary is fixed or how the cable net is lifted up. An obvious example for such structures is a tent or marquee, another is a spider's web. In the early days, physical modelling was the only way to determine the form of the structure and how it would perform under loads. Crucially, Buro Happold have been at the forefront of the development of computer programs that analyse tension structures, determine their form and provide geometric information for fabrication. Over the years, as the technology was applied in real projects, the results of those projects fed back into the development of the software, with each serving to advance the other.

The whole point about lightweight structures is that gravity is less of an issue. Like suspension bridges, they are capable of spanning great distances, and because they use a minimum of material and are quick to construct, they are also very economical ways of covering large areas. Their beauty is in the fact that they are forms that can be free and expressive. What is an issue, in terms of engineering design, are the stresses imposed on such structures by wind, rain and snow. Defined as 'non-uniform applied loads', the changing nature of such forces requires careful analysis and modelling.

'More and more the engineering is becoming the only way that the artist in the architect can get his art expressed,' says senior designer Paul Westbury. 'As we reduce the amount of materials that we use to build things with, it becomes more difficult to use those materials and therefore the scientist or the engineer has to become involved. The use of minimum materials means that you have to put maximum analysis into it.'

Buro Happold had recently designed a tent that was about a quarter of the size of the Dome and which made use of the same principle: straight tensioned cables supporting a fabric cover. Ian Liddell was confident that the same idea would work if it was increased in scale. Unlike beams or compression members, which can have all sorts of associated structural problems, such as buckling, when the scale is increased, there are no equivalent problems with straight tensioned cable, in which structural performance is defined solely by the material of which it is made. The concept appeared utterly feasible and it was also an extremely economical type of design which could be rapidly constructed, a persuasive argument given the programme.

In Mike Davies' original concept sketch, of a structure 380 metres in diameter, there was one ring of twelve masts yielding enormous side

> *The structure appears simple, but the trick is you have to know it's going to work.*
>
> Ian Liddell, Buro Happold

spans. In the subsequent drawings that were presented to the Millennium Commission, the secretary of state and assembled heads of industry, the concept of two sets of masts was explored, with the inner set positioned quite close to the middle. The idea was that there would be a limited area in the centre of the Dome, with the space outside the masts devoted to the exhibition. Ian Liddell's response accordingly had a double row of masts, with 12 towards the centre and 24 round the perimeter. The cable structure comprised paired lines of radial cables, each spanning about 25 metres between nodes, with hangar cables coming down from the masts supporting each node point, or junction between cable lengths, and tie-down cables going to the bottom of each mast. The radial cables joined together at the centre; at the perimeter they were anchored directly to the ground, in the type of arrangement found on a typical marquee.

To form the cover, it was envisaged that panels of flat fabric would be tensioned between the cable net. Tensioning fabric reduces the amount of deflection under load. A very simple way of understanding this concept is to think of a washing line: if the line is barely tightened, when you hang washing on it, the weight of the washing will pull the line down. If you tighten the line, the stress in the line will resist the weight of the washing. For an idea of the degree of tensioning required in the Dome, a 'fun fact' analogy makes the point very graphically: you could support the weight of a jumbo jet on its roof, despite the fact that the fabric cover is less than 1mm thick.

The big roof
Throughout the hectic months of June and July 1996 the original scheme for the Dome was worked up in greater detail. A 'mark 2' version eventually emerged, the result of ongoing discussions between the engineers and the architects. After thorough computer analysis, this was accepted as the base design in August 1996.

One of the first changes was that the diameter of the Dome was reduced from 400 metres to 320 metres, after it was discovered that the original scheme actually overhung the site and got in the way of some existing riverbank support structure. The main masts were then moved outwards and the outer ring of masts was dropped, at the request of Richard Rogers Partnership, who felt that this arrangement both looked better and was potentially less compromising for the floor area. This was a return to the simplicity of the original 12-mast concept but tuned for maximum efficiency. With only a single set of masts, they had to be higher. The radial lines were no longer joined in the middle, but started from a central hub. Properly defined, the resulting structure was now a 'spherical cap' – the uppermost portion of a sphere whose theoretical centre was deep underground.

Further refinements concerned the tie-down cables. The tie-down cables are designed to resist wind loads. When the wind blows, it produces an upward force on a roof. Tie-down cables, running from the underside of the cable-net structure to the ground, literally hold the roof down and prevent it from blowing off. Early on, it was realized that tie-down cables were unnecessary in the centre because the radial cables were so close together; they were only required at the edge where the panels of fabric were wider. But since the masts reached the ground, the tie-down cables also had to reach the ground, and in this position they interrupted the Dome's floor area. As it was important that the planned internal structures should be as clear of cables as possible, it was decided to raise the masts up 10 metres, on pyramid bases, thus lifting the tie-down cables away from the floor surface as well.

In its refined form, the structure consisted of 72 radial lines of cable starting from a ring in the middle and going to the perimeter edge, a distance of 150 metres. Each of the twelve masts supported six lines of radial cables. The radials were held in place by circumferential cables. At each of the connection points between a radial and circumferential cable – the node point – there was a hangar cable to the top of the mast. The hangar cables going to the furthest extremes of each set of six radial cables slightly pull inwards. The circumferential cables are designed to counter this inward pull and hold the radials in their correct position. The more the radial cables are tensioned or stretched, the more they pull down on the hangar cables, and thus the more the hangar cables are themselves tensioned. With tension stressing against tension, the structure becomes stiffer and more resistant to being deflected by load.

The beauty of cable-net structures is that they have tremendous load-sharing capacity. In engineering terms, they are 'highly redundant', which means failure of a single element does not compromise the whole. The pairing of the radial cables was designed to enhance this redundancy further. Again, reference to the spider's web can be helpful. When an insect is snared in a web, or breaks one of its strands, the entire web does not come to pieces.

This structural minimalism results in a very economic use of material. Just how economic can be gauged by the fact that the Dome – all the cables, all the fabric and all the masts – weighs about the same as a 12-metre cube of water. 'Being circular, the Dome is highly repetitive in terms of construction and it's highly efficient structurally,' explains Mike Davies. 'It could be seen as analagous to six nesting suspension bridges – it's no accident that the suspension bridge is the most efficient and lowest-cost way of achieving great spans.'

While the concept was essentially a simple one, the structure as a whole is extremely intricate and complex. In order to analyse it and ensure that it would work, not only in principle but also in practice, Buro Happold used a computer program called Tensyl, software which they had developed over a period of twenty years for analysing tension structures. A particular concern was the design of the huge masts, which would have to resist loads from wind and ice, as well as resist buckling. The results of the Tensyl analyses gave peak loads the components would have to bear, and the components were then sized accordingly. Subsequently, wind tunnel testing was also carried out.

The cigar shape of the masts is a classic profile for a 'member in compression' or what engineers refer to as a 'strut'. It is no accident that the Skylon, that memorably iconic feature of the Festival of Britain in 1951, was the same shape. In the case of the Dome, the hangar cables are pulling down at the top of each mast, putting a 'push' or compression into the mast. The problem with compression members – in this case the masts – is that they tend to buckle before the limit of the material has been reached, in the same way that a wooden ruler bends before it snaps. Widening the masts in the middle stabilizes them against buckling, but there was also a limitation on the overall diameter of the masts imposed by transportation requirements. A great deal of computer calculation went into verifying the precise load capacity.

'You've got to believe that it's going to work,' says Ian Liddell. 'There was no way we could put forward a design that wasn't going to work. Engineers are not allowed to do that. Engineers designing buildings have to make them work first time. If you are designing products you can do a lot more trialling than you can on buildings. On buildings you move forward in fairly small steps.'

In all its essentials, the big roof idea was to remain unchanged throughout the process of design development that followed. Compared to the completed Dome, however, the early proposals for the scheme do reveal some interesting differences. The circular form of the structure irresistibly suggested a clock face and an internal subdivision in the form of twelve equal slices. The designers were keen to express this layout on the outside of the structure and came up with the idea of transparent interpanels, which would highlight the structural masts and provide a striking way of announcing the position of the planned twelve entry-exit points round the perimeter. And the glittery spheres of the Circle of Time were still positioned round the Dome, at the clockface positions.

Design development

Design development is essentially a process of ensuring an idea will work: that a scheme fits the site, functions properly and generates the right quality of space. At the same time, design development also offers the opportunity for refinement, a paring away of what is superfluous, so

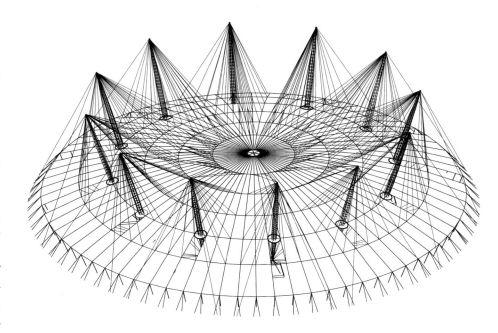

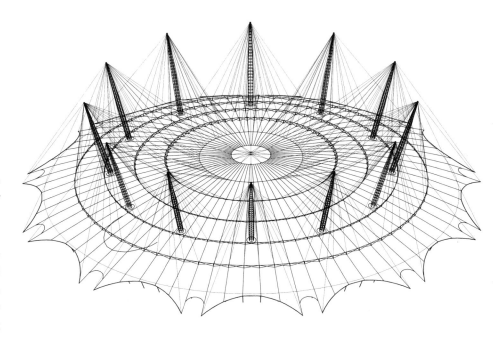

In the early stages of the design, before the treatment of the perimeter edge of the Dome had been finalized, it was envisaged that the radial cables would be pegged out all the way round the circumference, like a tent *(top)*. In the final design, however, scallops were introduced to refine the edge, to provide access points and to complete the aesthetic *(above)*.

that the original concept can be clearly expressed. Some changes were obvious fairly early on; others evolved in a long process of deliberation right up to the final placing of the steelworks order.

Vast structures like the Dome shift in and out of focus. Up close, it is the details – the nuts and bolts, fixings and connections – that provide a graspable, almost tangible, way in which the structure can be read. Given the unprecedented nature of the structure, many of these details could not simply be lifted from a pre-existing kit of parts, but had to be custom-designed.

In the original proposal, the edge of the Dome's roof was raised 10 metres off the ground. Each line of radial cables was anchored at a perimeter mast, and each of these 72 perimeter masts had a tie-back cable holding it in place. With the radials 'pegged out' all the way round the circumference, this would have produced a very different-looking building, rather like a circus tent.

A good deal of preliminary design discussion concerned how to treat the edge of the structure. One idea was to put the Dome on a raised area of level ground – a 'berm' – and surround it with a boardwalk overlooking the river. The berm idea persisted for quite some time, until eventually it was realized that it would take several months to bring in the soil; it also proved impossible to resolve the main entry and two-level visitor flows. Then Mike Davies suggested that they looked at bringing the roof right down to the ground and putting in external boundary cables. This proposal enclosed the perimeter masts, did away with the awkward tie-back cables, and made the whole structure more immediately accessible, allowing for larger openings to admit light and air into the interior.

'Richard Rogers Partnership were keen to articulate the edge a lot more and produce an area where it was easier to get large door openings,' says Paul Westbury. 'Between us we developed the system of a large boundary cable in a scallop form that intercepted the middle four of each of the six radial cables and transferred the force in those four intermediate radial cables to an anchor position at either end.'

At each of the 24 anchor positions, there is one radial line of cables, one scallop cable and one backstay to each of the twelve structural masts. (Each of the masts has two backstays, as well as two forestays which go to the centre.) The resultant pull is upwards and inwards. The upwards component of the force is resisted by the vertical anchors whose foundations extend some 24 metres into the ground. Inwards pull is resisted by a massive concrete compression ring that runs round the whole circumference of the Dome.

It is not enough for the structure to work, it must also be seen to be working. The architects wanted the structure to be expressive, which meant designing various elements in such a way as to reveal clearly the

job they were doing. The form of the anchor blocks, which resemble giant irons or anvils, represents precisely this type of refinement: while their shape is exact and considered, almost streamlined, they also look substantial and weighty, more than up to their structural role. As Glyn Trippick explains: 'Not only does the anchor block have to do the engineering work that we want, RRP were keen that it looked good as well. That's where this project needs both of us. It needs RRP to actually provoke us into producing details that look elegant.'

Another key refinement had to do with what was happening at the centre. The 72 lines of radial cables, each of which is actually a pair of cables, start from a ring in the middle. Originally this was going to be a single steel fabrication. During the tender period, but before the steelwork contracts were finally placed, concerns grew about the safety of this central ring. If it were to fail or fracture – and it was carrying a massive load of 700 tonnes – the whole roof would come apart and collapse. The answer was to replace the single steel ring with a cable ring, composed of twelve individual cables, two rows of six, one above the other, clamped together at the 72 radial positions. The inherent safety of this design is again based on the 'redundancy' principle: up to six of the cables can fail without compromising the safety of the roof.

Safety was also a concern when it came to the arrangement of the circumferential cables. Normally, in cable-net structures, cables running in one direction are clamped directly to cables running in the other direction so that they lie in the same plane. In the case of the Dome, given that the fabric cladding and the cable net would lie in the same plane, there was concern that the circumferential cables would act as a barrier or dam to snow or water, increasing the tendency for what engineers call 'ponding'. Ponding, or the build-up of surface water or snow, tends to lead to more ponding, until a point is reached where the load is so great that the fabric bursts. It was this type of problem that had resulted in the failure of a fabric-clad structure in Montreal.

To a certain extent, the tapering slope of the fabric panels of the Dome would help to act against ponding, but the Dome's engineers were nevertheless keen to raise the circumferential cables so that the risk was absolutely minimized. They developed a system of 'wishbones', rigid steel members, which hold the node point in place and lift the circumferential cables about 2.5 metres above the line of the fabric. Cross cables in between hold the wishbones in place. Delicate-looking from a distance, up close this is an enormous piece of metal assembly.

Buro Happold's experience with cable and fabric structures had also indicated that it was crucially important for an allowance to be made for rotation where cables are connected. If the end of a cable was connected with a normal straight pin, there was the risk that the cable might be bent during installation, in which case it would have had to

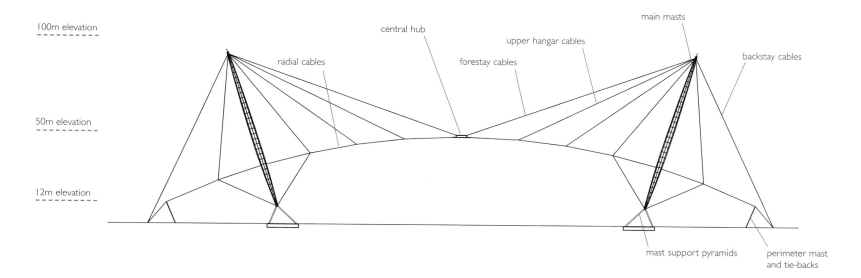

Early engineering drawings reveal the basic structural principles of the Dome, with the cable net held in space by hangar cables coming down from the masts *(above)*. The 'cigar' shape of the masts is designed to resist buckling *(below right)*.

have been replaced. For this reason, barrel pins were specified which allowed for movement in both vertical and horizontal planes.

Another difficulty was how to develop a workable system of connecting all the cables to the masts. Twenty-three separate cables have to connect into each masthead with a common intersection point. These connections, which would eventually be made by hand, also had to be readily accessible by someone working at the giddy height of 100 metres. During the initial design stage, Buro Happold positioned a series of flanges or lugs at the top and bottom of each mast; as details were worked up later by the steel contractor some of these connector plates were extended outwards to prevent individual cable lines from clashing with each other.

Decisions were also made very early on in the design process about how to connect the perimeter wall to the roof. Originally, the 72 small perimeter masts, which support the end of each radial cable, were intended to be outside the structure, but as the design developed the roof was brought down and the wall was moved out to enclose them.

The wall system the designers devised consists of vertical bowstring trusses, spanning between the ground and horizontal trusses on top, which are in turn connected to lugs on top of the perimeter masts. The bowstring form of the vertical trusses allowed a choice to be made between either cladding them on the curved or the vertical surface. Not surprisingly, the more dynamic curved option was the architects' choice.

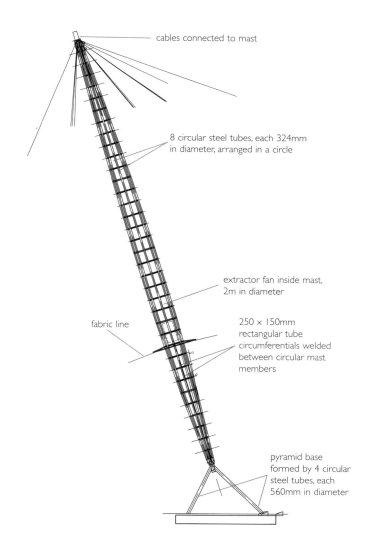

The end of the beginning

During the period when the Dome evolved from a scribbled sketch to a developed design that could be costed and programmed, the project as a whole was undergoing momentous sea changes. Money was at the heart of the issue. Following the Millennium Commission's decision to choose Greenwich, the Imagination proposal was no longer financially viable as the funding provided by the Birmingham NEC would not be available. If the unthinkable were to happen, and the project failed, there was no longer sufficient equity to cover the potential losses.

From February to May 1996, the Millennium Commission tried to find a major corporation who would be prepared to stand behind the Greenwich scheme. The choice of the Greenwich site had opened up new possibilities in terms of investment. After all, there were many facilities that London lacked, facilities such as an all-day visitor attraction or a major conference centre which could offer the potential for long-term development.

Despite such incentives, the financial circles simply could not be squared. At the beginning of the summer, British Airways, the last corporation in contention, eventually conceded that they could not make a commercial case for backing the project.

At the mid-year point, with no viable financial backing forthcoming, the Commission found itself in the unenviable position of having to make a decision on whether to go ahead with the project or to pull it. What was complicating matters enormously was a certain fraying of political will. With a general election due to be held at some point in the following year, the summer of 1996 saw the beginning of a long campaign run-up. Although the Opposition had always been represented by a nominee on the Commission, there was now an increased need for everything to be seen to be done with Labour's knowledge and consent, given that there was more than a passing chance that the party would form the next administration.

In the face of this seeming impasse, the government demonstrated their commitment by saying that they would ensure that the Millennium Commission had sufficient Lottery money to act as 'the underwriter of last resort'; in other words, that there would be guaranteed funding to provide equity if the worst were to happen and the project failed. The crucial implication of this commitment was that the company,

> *It was a project that refused to die. This project ought to have died about ten times in 1996, let alone subsequently.*
>
> Jennie Page, NMEC

Millennium Central Ltd, set up by Imagination Ltd to run the project, would now be to all intents and purposes operating within the public sector. At this stage, however, before the extent of the budget for the new scheme had been established, it was still envisaged that the company would remain a private company.

At the same time, Colin Marshall and Bob Ayling of British Airways said that they would be happy to spearhead the appeal for sponsorship. In June 1996, Michael Heseltine, a long-time supporter of the project, and one of the two government commissioners at the time, organized a meeting at the Cabinet Office to which leading businessmen were invited. On presentation of the Dome, site and content concepts by the designers, and with the clear commitment of the Commission, he managed to obtain sufficient expressions of interest that the Commission could feel confident that double the amount of cash 'up front' could be raised – £150 million as against the £75 million originally projected.

In August 1996 Buro Happold produced a concept report on the design of the Dome, together with a proposed programme. As Ian Liddell remembers: 'Everyone immediately locked onto the big roof idea.' From the start, the Dome had an immensely unifying effect on the whole project; it literally tied it down under its vast cover and made it seem achievable for the first time.

These developments served to galvanize the project into action. The Commission, which had already provided some development funding to Imagination, now undertook to provide enough cash to step up the design momentum and allow a planning application to be submitted to Greenwich in the autumn: Richard Rogers Partnership was asked to prepare the scheme for planning, with Buro Happold assisting. British Airways undertook to find a chief executive for the company that was to be set up to run the project. At the same time the chief executive designate (the eventual appointee was Barry Hartop) was given the task of coming up with a business plan, together with a significant section of the design work in detail by the Commission meeting in December.

For the engineers, the programme was more of an immediate worry. Working backwards, Buro Happold had said in their August report that it would be necessary to go out to tender for the steel and cables by the end of 1996 if the structure were to be ready by September 1998, which was when Imagination estimated that the Dome should be finished. This would allow the masts and cable net to be put up before the next winter, ready to be covered with fabric early the following year to make the structure weatherproof.

Steve Bell's reaction to the Dome, from *The Guardian*, 1 November 1996.

The autumn of 1996 was a period of feverish activity, as the design was developed in sufficient detail to go out to tender for the steelwork. W. S. Atkins, a civil engineering firm acting as consultants to English Partnerships on the Greenwich masterplan, were asked to project-manage the scheme. Buro Happold, working with Peter English, a civil engineer then working as a consultant with W. S. Atkins, drafted the conditions of the contracts and put the tender documentation together, knowing that these tenders would have to go out before planning approval had even been gained. This step, which represented a huge vote of confidence in the project's future, was actually based on pure pragmatism. 'If we hadn't have done that, it wouldn't have gone out to tender until June 1997 and then it wouldn't have happened,' says Ian Liddell simply. 'I never thought the project would be cancelled, because it was something that could be realized. It was a very practical solution.'

Peter English explains the thinking behind the programme: 'We had to get the masts erected in October 1997 and the fabric on in the spring of 1998 in order to achieve that date of September 1998 when the building would be waterproof. Working back from there, that meant that we had to have the foundations completed by then, which meant starting the foundations around July. But we also had to have the masts available which meant we had to have them built, delivered to site and erected by the end of October, which working back again, meant we ought to be placing an order at about the end of February.'

Submitting the scheme to Greenwich Council for approval in October 1996 initiated a planning process that would become

Byzantine in its complexity. The precise nature of the exhibition and how much funding would be available were still unknown, but ideas for the Dome were rapidly taking shape. During the public consultation phase, the simplicity of the Dome and the power of its image was a huge asset when it came to explaining the project, a time-consuming process that involved a great many public meetings, all attended by Mike Davies and Barry Hartop, as well as meetings with local interest groups. No less persuasive in winning hearts and minds was the initial exhibition launching the scheme put on at Greenwich Town Hall by Imagination.

'Imagination carried it along for a year,' says Ian Liddell. 'They carried the whole idea and without them doing that the thing would have died. They created all these images and ideas and produced an amazing exhibition in Greenwich for the planning permission which explained the whole idea. That was with the Dome in it, of course. In January 1996 before Imagination was selected they had to present their proposal at the Millennium Commission. . . . There were two groups presenting and Imagination was given this little room, like a meeting room, all done out in cream and floral carpet, a real Whitehall special. "We can't use this," was Gary Withers' reaction, so he and the Imagination team transformed it. He completely panelled the room out in white, installed new lighting, and hung his exhibition inside it. Typical Gary job. He did the same at Greenwich Town Hall for the exhibition. Completely rebuilt the interior.'

The shadow of uncertainty

Throughout the long deliberation about the nature of the festival, the process of selecting a site and the conception of the Dome, the project had encountered a few low points, narrowly missing being mired in them; any problems had ultimately proved surmountable. There was a scheme, representing an elegant solution to the difficulties of both site and programme, that had been submitted for planning permission, and the design had been developed in sufficient detail to go out for tender. The site was in the process of remediation; the long-term strategies were taking shape. An air of excitement was beginning to surround the entire project. What then happened, however, ushered in a protracted period of uncertainty. From December 1996 until six months later, no one involved in the project was to be sure from one day to the next whether it would go ahead.

Alarm bells first rang at the December Commission meeting. It was the business plan. At over £750 million before risk or contingency had been taken into account, and with the possibility that the final bill would top £1 billion, the budget was patently excessive. Its rejection signalled the end of Barry Hartop's involvement.

The design team was finding itself under immense strain. On the one hand, the public nature of the project now entailed tremendous levels of government scrutiny and imposed the requirement for complete and utter transparency. On the other hand, there was the need to satisfy the commercial sponsors, who had been asked to provide more money. Imagination, who carried the responsibility for producing the exhibition, had begun to express concerns about their ability to deliver something that would both meet the aspirations of the Commission and satisfy the sponsors. 'The task was intolerable,' says Jennie Page. 'I don't think anyone should ever underestimate just how appalling the problems were in those early days.'

As Mike Davies remembers: 'Gary's view was "I know what it takes to make this show work", which is more to do with gut creative feel than bearing in mind what it's like to be scrutinized by the eagle eyes of six hundred MPs. His contribution was enormously valuable in those early days. We found him a delight to work with. . . . The spirit of what he was doing was right and the spirit of what he was doing is actually right here now.' Yet despite the brilliance of Imagination's ideas, there was a general belief that the existing organizational structure of the project was simply not going to work. It was a time of intense concern for all parties, not least the Commission.

At this crunch point, Jennie Page, since 1995 the Chief Executive of the Millennium Commission, was asked to look further at the budget, along with Claire Sampson, one of her in-house team, and a group of external advisors led by Jeff Hawkins, formerly advising the Millennium Commission, and who would eventually be brought in as the director of programme and projects. Over the period of Christmas and New Year this team went in and stripped out the budget. Their preliminary conclusion was that the project could probably be achieved, including risk money, for a figure of somewhere between £600 million and £800 million. 'The architects were extremely concerned to ensure that we didn't end up with what was known as the "blasted heath", in other words that we didn't strip out so much other than the Dome that we had got a site at Greenwich that was terribly unwelcoming and unattractive,' says Jennie Page.

When Greenwich Council announced that it had resolved to grant planning permission to the scheme in January 1997, what should have been good news was clouded by increasing political difficulties. There had always been the real risk that the project would get becalmed in the political doldrums as the election approached, but the scale of the budget, even after pruning, was raising huge financial question marks

> *Jennie's one of the great chess players, no question about it. I think she's pulled off magic in many areas.*
>
> **Mike Davies, Richard Rogers Partnership**

Where did he get that hat?
A competitor in the London Marathon
runs with the millennium theme.

over the whole scheme. With the election now only months away, establishing the position of the Opposition became even more critical; it was widely assumed that if Labour came to power, an eventuality that was looking increasingly likely, the project would be killed.

On 13 January 1997, the Millennium Commission agreed that satisfactory terms and conditions would be achievable with the revised draft budget, and offered a grant of £200 million, to be made available once the budget and business plan were developed in greater detail. It was also made clear that if the budget could be brought down to within the estimated figure, the Commission wanted Jennie Page to move across and run what would now be a new company, operating under a tighter level of central control. One of the conditions of continuing with the project was that Millennium Central Ltd should be reincorporated as a 'non-departmental public body' or NDPB. NDPBs are governed by corporate law but at the same time subject to the scrutiny of Parliament: it was a shift that brought a new level of accountability to the entire project.

With the revised budget falling somewhere between £600 million and £800 million, the Millennium Commission's grant would not be sufficient. The Commission were scheduled to cease receiving Lottery revenue on 31 December 2000 and had made it clear that they could not make extra money available to the project since this would compromise existing programmes. However, the Commission had also made it clear that they were willing to act as a conduit for extra funding, if the government could find a means to make it available.

At this critical juncture, significant talks between government and Opposition took place: what was at stake was an extra year's Lottery revenue – an extension of the Commission's funding life – to underpin the business plan of the new company. Then a carefully crafted Commons statement was prepared which made many things explicit for the first time. In the statement, delivered on 20 January by the secretary of state, Virginia Bottomley, the government said it would bring forward an Order under the National Lottery Act 1993 to extend the funding life of the Commission, that the new company would be a public body with all the existing shares of the shell company set up by Imagination to run the project, Millennium Central Ltd, taken into public ownership, that Bob Ayling would continue as the company's chairman with Jennie Page running it and, crucially, that this was being done with the agreement of the Opposition who retained 'the right to review the business plan'. It was a go-ahead, but qualified by the proviso of the review: cancellation further down the line remained a possibility.

On 12 February 1997, Millennium Central Ltd became operational as a public sector company and its shares were transferred to a single government Shareholder. Initially on two months' secondment, Jennie

Page, Claire Sampson, the head of exhibition and festival of the Commission, Jeff Hawkins and their junior staff began working on the creation of a business plan ready for the incoming government. A short-term interim grant agreement was negotiated with the Commission that enabled the new company to spend £12 million and progress with the project as if the likely answer of the new government's review would be 'yes'. This grant was conditional on the company undertaking to keep the cost of closure within a further £12 million. Richard French of W. S. Atkins and the newly appointed construction managers, a team led by Bernard Ainsworth, persuaded the contractors – such as Keller Ground Engineering (piling), Watson Steel (masts and cables) and Koch Hightex (PVC fabric) – to commit to developing the project on a semi-speculative basis.

> *The whole way in which the company grew was predetermined by this continuing shadow of uncertainty.*
>
> Jennie Page, NMEC

In the spring, two other key figures joined the new company: David Trench, appointed the new site and structures director, and Ken Robinson, brought in to run operations. Essentially self-employed, both were willing to take on the risk of working on a project with an unknown future. David Trench's arrival and the refocus of the company at this stage led to a reduction in W. S. Atkins' role and a reconfiguring of the team. The prevailing situation, however, made it impossible to recruit other senior members of staff from existing jobs, notably a senior commercial director or a senior finance director. 'I stopped everything,' says Ken Robinson. 'I closed my businesses – it's cost me a fortune. I resigned all my directorships. I'm only doing this because it's the most wonderful responsibility and opportunity to use everything that I've assimilated all my life.'

By March, more detailed figures were beginning to emerge. As expected, it now looked as though an additional £200 million would be required from the Commission, together with a provision of around £50 million in cash flow, which would bring the level of the Lottery grant up to £449 million. To this would be added £150 million in sponsorship, together with projected commercial income, based on estimates of visitor numbers. The budget was beginning to settle in its final shape.

It was still far from clear, however, what would happen on the other side of the election. 'From 1996 to the middle of 1997 when we didn't know whether the project was going to happen or not, we went through a whole series of reviews, any of which could have killed it,' says Gregor Harvie. 'At any of those points we could have gone in in the morning and been told, "Don't come back tomorrow." That went on for a period of six to eight months, when it could have been the last day,

every day.' The letting of the steel contracts, roof contracts, the recruitment of the construction managers were all undergone with these uncertainties still hanging over everyone's heads. During this time, the company also commissioned a piece of qualitative market research to re-examine what the millennium actually meant to people. The results suggested that beneath the surface criticism and the desire simply to have a party, most people wanted the millennium to mark a change for the better. 'Time to Make a Difference' emerged as the new theme for the exhibition, with corresponding implications for the design of the exhibition – the Dome's contents.

Go-ahead

On 1 May 1997, Britain elected its first Labour government in 18 years, in a landslide victory that redrew the political map. Those working on the Dome held their breath as the promised government review got under way. The project was approaching the point of no return.

The review, agonizingly, took its time, although Whitehall repeatedly assured the project's creators that it was breaking all records to come up with an answer. As the project built up its own momentum and preparatory site works got under way, the pressure of time meant that

it was becoming extremely difficult to make value-for-money decisions. Media, if not political, scrutiny was at its peak, with the press clamouring for a decision and, largely, agitating for that decision to be negative. Opinions were evenly split among those who were working on the project, between those who fully expected that Labour, as a party keen to impress the voters with its fiscal rectitude, would kill it, and those who held a more optimistic view that a bold vision would prevail. On 11 June, the Commission's own appraisal of the business case had confirmed that the exhibition should be taken forward. These results were made available to the government reviewers.

> **IT'S DOMESDAY**
> *Daily Mirror*, 18 June 1997
> **DUMP THAT DOME**
> *Sun*, 18 June 1997

David Trench was one of the sceptics. As he recalls: 'There was a lot of faith that it would go ahead but not with me. I didn't think it could possibly go ahead. I thought the government had every chance to pull up stumps. They were very keen to impress upon the business world that they were going to continue the fiscal policies of the previous government. And it had become a much higher risk venture since so much time had been lost off the programme. No one was more surprised than me on the 19th.'

This is a date that is etched on the mind of everyone associated with the project. To the obvious surprise of many people, the answer on 19 June 1997 was: 'Yes'. As Jennie Page recalls, 'I still don't believe they would have done it on 19 June, which was a Thursday, the day of a Cabinet meeting, had it not been for the fact that I'd said to them, well, actually, we're sending the piling rigs in on the 23rd, which was the Monday...'. The uncertainty, at last, was finally over.

The new government had its own conditions to impose, conditions that would affect the entire nature of the project, from design right through to construction. The result of the review, taken it must be remembered at a time when the Dome's steel contracts and roof contracts had already been let, was that the project would go ahead on the basis that it would result in no extra burden on the taxpayer; it would be a truly national event; it would entertain and inspire; the management of the project would be strengthened by involving the best business and creative talent; and it would leave a lasting legacy.

While the timescale had always been more than understood, the budget was now firmly fixed. The review also re-emphasized the 'legacy' condition. Up to this point, design work had proceeded on the assumption that the Dome need only be a temporary structure, with a short life of at best a couple of years. Now it was clear that it should itself form part of the project's legacy to the surrounding area. It is to the credit of the Dome's designers that this repositioning was to have only one major consequence – the change in the choice of roof fabric.

New government, new branding. To signal the project's secure future, Millennium Central Ltd was renamed the New Millennium Experience Company (NMEC). The project as a whole – the Dome, its contents and associated millennium projects – became the Millennium Experience. This renaming, however, was not merely a cosmetic change, but marked a new forward-looking direction for the project and a new aim of encouraging active participation.

Although the uncertainty was over at last, the months of struggle had taken their toll. A casualty of the long period of redefinition and development was the loss of Imagination. 'Imagination behaved impeccably,' says Jennie Page. 'It was just quite clear that it wasn't working.' The departure of Imagination was to have its own implications for the development of the Millennium Experience.

The first of many visits: Bernard Ainsworth, manager of the McAlpine Laing Joint Venture, shows recently elected Prime Minister Tony Blair around the site, accompanied by John Prescott, Chris Smith and Peter Mandelson.

On site

Following the results of the government review in June 1997, Greenwich Council formally issued the scheme with planning permission and within days of 19 June English Partnerships had signed an agreement lease that gave the New Millennium Experience Company phased possession of the exhibition site. From this point onwards, things began to happen very fast. Almost immediately, the piling rigs went in, driving the first of 8,000 piles into the peninsula ground, a task they would complete in record time three months later. With little more than two years left, the race was on to beat the clock.

In normal building projects, the start of site works signals the conclusion of the design phase as responsibility shifts to the contractor charged with construction. In the case of the Dome, design work did not stop with the move to site but began to run in parallel and be integrated with a huge number of other dynamic processes. This compression, brought about by the scale and complexity of the project, its unique nature and the exceptionally tight timescale, brought with it the potential for both triumph and disaster. 'In a project of this size there is endless scope for misunderstanding which has to be hammered out on site and you can't do that at a distance,' says Jennie Page.

Integrating the design and construction phases was the only way to achieve the best programme. There was the chance that such integration would streamline decision-making, but there was equally the risk of muddle and confusion, with people constantly tripping over each other's toes. Managing the process called for a new contractual arrangement to bind everyone together and direct heroic efforts towards that fast-approaching goal.

A not insignificant side benefit of the project's scale was that it was economically feasible to move the entire team of client, architects, engineers and construction managers down to

The site office brought the client, architects, engineers and construction team together to streamline communication *(top)*. Jennie Page, chief executive of NMEC, stands inside a mast section, flanked by Ian Liddell and Mike Davies *(above)*. The momentum of construction gave the project drive and cohesion *(left)*.

the site and install them in the same building. This was a site hut with a difference: a two-storey, 2,700-square-metre prefabricated office, fully equipped with £1 million's worth of information technology, including 85 CAD stations and a video link to NMEC's main headquarters in Buckingham Palace Road, Victoria. At this nerve centre the team members were brought face to face, where they could sort out potential differences and come up with solutions on the spot, rather than at the chilly distance of a fax or letter. On site, the formal distinctions between one company and another – the headed-notepaper mentality – suddenly began to matter less. And as the structure took shape, with the great masts visible from the windows of the site office, the project acquired an unstoppable momentum of its own. 'It was absolutely important that we had all the resources here,' says site and structures director David Trench. 'This was so fast we had to get all the decision makers together. I insisted that there should be totally devoted and dedicated teams on site with a partner capable of making decisions. . . . I have never worked with such intellectual rigour around me.'

It was real and it was fun. It was also gruelling. As Mike Davies reminded his team: 'Enjoy it now, because you'll look back on it all one day and realize that this was the project of a lifetime.' On site, the atmosphere was infectious and highly charged. People fell in love, played practical jokes, sent silly memos – and worked, often round the clock, and routinely from early morning to late at night. At senior level there were tempestuous meetings, titanic clashes of policy and direction, as strong personalities fought for what they passionately believed in. 'Two things in particular have struck me about this project,' says Mike Davies. 'The first is the large number of women in very senior roles, and I've noticed that when women are involved they tend to win. The second is that chocolate works. We're all chocoholics down here, I'm one, Jennie's one, Claire's one and Ken's one. When things get difficult in a meeting, out comes the chocolate and all of a sudden life is easier. We never go to major decision-making meetings now without chocolate. It's been one of the great glues on the project.'

Ultimately, however, what cannot be quantified, planned or predicted is how a group of people are going to work together. On site, the teamwork across the board – architects, engineers, client, construction management – became a real factor in the successful realization of the project. On its own, a 'beat the clock' mentality is not enough to generate this degree of creativity. Undoubtedly outside pressures – the very public nature of the project – had some part to play. In the end, perhaps, it was the nature of the project itself that created this vital cohesion. No one had done anything like this before. Everyone had to be innovative; in the process they could only rely on each other.

> *One of the most wonderful things has been the spirit on site. People have asked to be put on the job. They've worked very hard, but they've worked with pleasure.*
> Richard Rogers, Richard Rogers Partnership

Running the project

In the early days of the project, when NMEC consisted of only a skeleton staff, letters of enquiry would occasionally arrive hopefully addressed to: 'Jennie, The Dome, London', in a not wildly inaccurate assessment of the size of the company's operations. After the go-ahead, as the speed of developments accelerated, so did the levels of complexity. The scale of the challenge facing the new company was immense, as Jennie Page explains: 'Here is a company that has the largest building site in Europe under its control. Here is a company putting on 80,000 square metres of exhibition and the largest and possibly the most expensive show in the world. Here is a company proposing to bring 12 million visitors to site, start up from day one and close down a year later, and no one has ever done that anywhere in the world before. And it's the same company, and we're doing it simultaneously.'

The company's new Shareholder, the Rt Hon Peter Mandelson, MP, Minister without Portfolio, took on the role of one of the project's most enthusiastic – as well as highly visible – proponents. By temperament not a person likely to be content to mumble vague words of encouragement from the sidelines, he provided welcome political support, as well as assuming a more proactive role in the shaping of the project's direction than his predecessors had done. One result was that Sir Cameron Mackintosh was brought in to create the live show which was envisaged as the centrepiece of the Dome's attractions. The inevitable result of this was even more press attention. In David Trench's estimation: 'Mandelson is a visionary but he came with baggage. The press had their daggers into him. I think he saved the project, that was his biggest contribution.'

Notwithstanding the press exposure, the project was also operating under very high levels of government scrutiny. As a great public enterprise, it was essential that everything was done – and was seen to be done – on an open and equitable basis. Through the Culture, Media and Sport Select Committee and through individual Parliamentary Questions and general correspondence from MPs, every detail of the project became subject to the same searching level of enquiry. Requests for information on any point, no matter how minor, had to be answered in full – all while the project itself was still in the process of development. As time went by, the questions, both official and unofficial, ran into their hundreds: What plans were there to represent Winston Churchill's contribution to British history in the Dome? Could an assessment be provided for the ambient air temperature between the zones? Would genetically modified food be served in the Dome?

Jan Anderson, a secondee from the Department of Environment, Transport and Regions, joined the company in October 1997 to cope with the increasing demands imposed by public accountability. If the Dome was a gift for the press and a gift for environmental activists, it was also a gift for those riding their own political hobbyhorses: 'There's an expectation that every single detail of every single decision we make has to be declared. We don't have a problem with making details public, but where we feel somewhat concerned at times is that it is not always necessarily the case that the asker of the question has a keen interest in an issue, it is that the asker of the question has some political point to make.'

This extra layer of accountability, inherent in the public sector status of the company, added a 'bespoke twist' to the project. The biggest impact fell on Jennie Page, who as Chief Executive, had to attend regular meetings with the Shareholder and report monthly to the Millennium Commission, who had imposed their own terms and conditions on the award of the grant – a grant which, after all, did represent the biggest Lottery award ever made. In her capacity as Accounting Officer, personally responsible to Parliament for the use of the company's resources, Jennie Page also had to give evidence to the Select Committee whenever the project was reviewed. The pressure was constant. 'We're on the phone daily with the Commission about one thing or another,' says Jan Anderson.

All this was happening at a time when the largest construction site in Europe was in full swing, and when the exhibition was still at a critical

Peter Mandelson, Minister without Portfolio and NMEC's first Shareholder under the Labour government, tours Watson Steel near Bolton in 1997 to inspect progress on the construction of the Dome's masts *(left)*. Every aspect of constructing the Dome, not least earthworks, has been on a massive scale *(above)*.

The construction of the Dome has been marked by ferocious controversy. Photographed through a wire fence, here officials try to convince nine activists who scaled the crane used to erect the Dome's masts to come down to earth.

stage in its development. It would have been an impossible task had the Dome's inherent flexibility of design not served to ease the strain. Just as the structure provided a physical separation from its content, buying time to decide what these would be, constructing the Dome was an enterprise that could effectively be isolated from the core business of the company, which was to design, create and run the Millennium Experience.

As the months went by and construction milestones were met, the conspicuous success of the Dome gave the whole project an enormous boost of self-confidence. A steady stream of MPs, ministers, foreign dignitaries and officials were taken round the site to see for themselves what the most detailed answer to a Parliamentary Question or well-phrased press release could never hope to convey. Before a single ticket had been even sold, the Dome was already acting as a visitor attraction in its own right.

'What I like about this place is the huge mixture of people,' says Jan Anderson. 'You've got the suits, as you would expect in any finance outfit, but you've also got the completely individual production people, the artists and the creatives. It's an incredibly intriguing mixture of people – I can't think of a parallel. The management structure is very loose. A conventional structure would not work at all.'

The contractual route

Before the move to site, and before the results of the government review were even known, it was clear that some restructuring of the way the project was organized was becoming necessary. A certain amount of friction was developing over who would ultimately control the design process and, with all parties operating out of their own offices, it was easy for a degree of duplication to enter the management structure. Consultants to English Partnerships on the Greenwich masterplan, W. S. Atkins had also been asked to project-manage the Dome on behalf of its client, NMEC (then Millennium Central Ltd).

Peter English had been responsible for drawing up a brief for whoever would be engaged to manage the Dome's construction.

As anyone who has ever hired a team of builders for the simplest home improvement scheme could tell you, the twin risks associated with any building project are overrunning the schedule and exceeding the budget. In the Dome, neither could be allowed to happen. Quite early on in the planning of the project, it had been decided to opt for a relatively new contractual route, pioneered originally in the United States and implemented since the late 1980s in some major British schemes. This route was formally defined as 'construction management', a rather opaque term that clouds the essential simplicity and elegance of the idea. Instead of the client appointing a contractor to run a project and the contractor in turn appointing subcontractors to carry out specialist work, all the contracts with trade contractors and consultants are directly with the client itself, with the construction manager managing every aspect of the scheme, including the design, on the client's behalf. This streamlined legal framework has very significant benefits. It allows the design and construction phases to be overlapped and it effectively puts the contractor on the client's side rather than setting up adversarial roles. In February 1997 a joint venture between two of Britain's leading construction firms, Sir Robert McAlpine and Laing, won the bid to be the 'construction manager' of the Dome.

On the client side, a very important early appointment had been that of David Trench, who arrived in April 1997 to take up the role of site and structures director. As the person who had been brought in to drive the massively overrun and overspent British Library through to final completion, David Trench was keen to implement some of the important lessons he had learned working on that scheme. In particular, he was determined to run the project on the basis of 'target-cost contracts' where the 'pain' and the 'gain' are shared by all those involved. This innovative form of contract effectively serves to remove any possible incentive for late running and minimizes the likelihood of defensive barriers being set up between consultants, where each has a tendency to blame the other when something goes wrong and costs can soar out of control.

In the contractual arrangements set up on the Dome, the three principal consultants, Richard Rogers Partnership, Buro Happold and McAlpine Laing were bound together. If the project were to come in under budget, all three would share a bonus. If it were to be late, all three would face the same penalty. That meant that everyone had a vested interest in getting the project built on time and to budget and a real incentive to help each other achieve that aim. With these new contractual arrangements, the management structure was stripped to its bare essentials and the need for additional project management was no

Hoovering round the model of the Body zone, in one of its early manifestations *(left)*.

Successive press launches, revealing the latest plans for the content of the Dome, have been part of the process of keeping the public informed about progress. The launch in February 1998, where initial proposals for six zones were presented, brought together many of the Dome's leading political supporters, including Peter Mandelson and Michael Heseltine *(above right)*. The Prime Minister inspects a model of the Dome *(below)*.

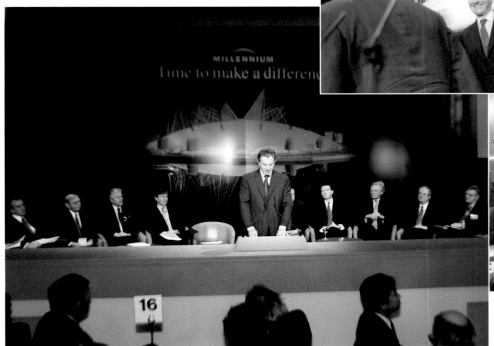

Jennie Page demonstrates the internal arrangement of the Dome's content with the aid of the 'pizza plan', a coloured plan of the layout.

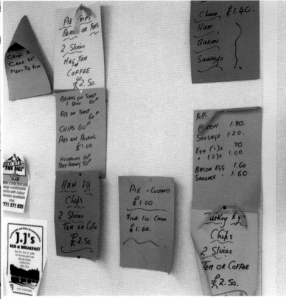

Christmas in the site canteen. One of the most striking aspects of the construction of the Dome has been the positive site relations, a 'can-do' attitude shared by managers and workers alike. Good site conditions — catering, showers and other facilities — made an important contribution.

longer required. Accordingly, W. S. Atkins left the project, while remaining the consultants for the masterplan as a whole.

'The contractual structure is absolutely crucial because it does mean that people have got a common interest,' says Jennie Page. 'The way that David has managed the site has been masterly, and the McAlpine Laing Joint Venture has been excellent in terms of making sure that the on-site relations are good.'

Managing the site

'It's amazing what people can do if you release them rather than imprison them,' says David Trench, responsible for the Dome's site and structures as well as its transport infrastructure. With a vast number of very complicated procedures all more or less happening at once, the scope for human error was immense. Keeping the lines of communication open and reducing any formalities to the minimum was essential to win the trust and motivation of everyone on site, from the construction workers to the managers.

Bernard Ainsworth led the eighty-strong McAlpine Laing Joint Venture team on site. Both companies had strong family cultures which helped to create a seamless integration of management and production skills. 'A joint venture is a fantastic way of putting a team together for a big job. You've got two pools to fish from.'

One of the Joint Venture's first tasks was to put a price on the Dome, to translate a 'global' budget into real figures and sell this vision to all parties. 'We had to work out what a big tent in the middle of Greenwich was going to cost, filled with we didn't know what. Bernard Thomas, our cost planner, put a huge amount of thought into calculating the final cost of a scheme not yet designed.' This critical task began immediately and by May 1997 a realistic breakdown was beginning to emerge that people could believe in and commit to. When the project was given the go-ahead, an enormously complex process of planning, procurement and cost control got under way. 'I don't think any of us really understood how big a thing it was, either in terms of physical size or in terms of the amount we were meant to be doing in the time.'

The target-cost contracts were an effective way of marrying agendas and providing a clear sense of direction. But there were other contributing factors, not least the personalities who made up each team and their willingness to work with and trust each other. 'It's all about people having comfort levels with each other,' says Bernard Ainsworth. 'All of us have the technical knowledge and we've all been in the construction industry twenty, thirty years and all at the top end. If you get the people factor right, suddenly you have this synergy and it's almost self-energizing after that.'

The open-plan arrangement of the site office was an important means of generating this degree of trust. While Richard Rogers Partnership and Buro Happold were used to working in open-plan offices, McAlpine Laing had to be persuaded of its merits. Bernard Ainsworth was adamant that there should be no 'little boxes' for people to retreat into. With a shared reception and everyone linked by computer there were no visible boundaries between one company and the next. Informality was a crucial way of challenging defensiveness and served to speed up the entire process. If there was a difficult decision to make, which involved the architect, the engineer, the construction manager and the client, within half an hour all four could put their heads together and hammer out a solution.

'The construction industry is littered with letters,' says Bernard Ainsworth. 'There's constant backside covering. If you get a letter on headed paper, you immediately feel you have to reply to it. If you get a note that confirms a conversation, it immediately becomes less emotive. It's better still if you can speak face to face.'

David Trench shares the same philosophy: 'This is how I regard administration and procedures: they're shackles. I wanted to have a project where we freed people up to do what they're good at. I don't want forms, I don't want letters. I want management. There's a confusion that if you tick boxes you can run anything, which is a confusion between administration and management. What we've got here is a concentration on eyeball to eyeball, a concentration on talking, not writing, and a concentration on doing and not talking. It's also a philosophy of partnership, it's joint ownership, not employee/employer.'

Money and effort were spent making sure that the same attitude went right the way through the project, from the managerial level down to the site. There were awards and rewards: cakes in the shape of the Dome for the abseilers, T-shirts, Marks and Spencer's vouchers and other benefits for those with the best work rate or best safety record. With over 1,000 people working in often very difficult conditions, safety was a prime consideration. 'Safety is a culture,' says Bernard Ainsworth. 'This has been one of the few sites where people always have their helmets on, their protective glasses, their site boots.' Along with the

educational role of induction courses, the reward system reinforced positive action. And regularly handing out safety certificates – at the pub – also served as a convenient pretext to get everyone together and talking. It was an inclusive atmosphere. David Trench made sure that when one of the 'big days' was coming up, with an important presentation scheduled to be made to VIPs, he would make the same presentation to the workforce the day before, so that everyone felt part of the same effort.

As well as bonding sessions down the pub, the site conditions were exceptional, with three canteens, showers, lockers and a parking area. In the main site office itself, the same message of quality was reinforced. With carpeting on the floor, fresh flowers on the reception desk, and a buzzing creative atmosphere, it was a far cry from the usual muddy hut filled with tea-stained mugs. Good working conditions were a key part of the team's industrial relations strategy.

The majority of the seventy trade contracts on the Dome have been won by British firms, and wherever possible local labour has also been used: 50 per cent of the workforce has come from Greenwich and the Thames Gateway boroughs. The biggest risk on a project of this size was always the potential for a breakdown in industrial relations leading to leverage, a situation all too familiar on large public projects in the past. As Bernard Ainsworth explains: 'On other projects, walkouts were part of the ethos. We were determined to do things differently. At the outset we sat down with national union leaders and developed an agreement: we would offer good conditions and they would commit to a policy of communication. It was a bond of mutual trust.' As the project went on, many of the firms who started out with one contract went on to win two, three or four more, and a corresponding ease and trust was built up. Many trade contracts incorporated incentive systems of bonuses payable if targets were exceeded.

'At the end of the day, David is the client and he picks up the bill. He wants to get value for money, but value for money comes from a whole stack of different directions, it doesn't just come from lowest price,' says Bernard Ainsworth. David Trench agrees: 'Everyone brings a can-do attitude to it. All the contractors are not necessarily awarded a contract because they're the cheapest – although they've got to be pretty keen on price – they also have to have a belief in the project.'

One of the key early procurements was to secure the first fully serviced canteen for what would eventually become a thousand-person site. When the site was first occupied, but before the procurement stage had been reached, a local firm, TS Catering, was brought in to run a small canteen. 'TS Catering was really Teresa,' explains Bernard Ainsworth. 'And her food was fantastic, homemade apple pie, pork chops, bacon rolls, real cooking.' TS Catering was encouraged to bid for the catering

David Trench, responsible for site and structures, signing the underside of the capping piece at the centre of the Dome roof *(left)*. This detailed model of the Dome, made up by Richard Rogers Partnership, proved a valuable presentational tool *(below right)*.

contract and found itself on the final short list, in competition with a large organization with a long track record of handling site catering on this vast scale. 'We chose Teresa. First we sat down with her and explained the implications of running something this size, how to work the VAT, how to handle the National Insurance contributions and so on. She went away and thought it through, and then she accepted. It's been a stunning success.' Helping a small local firm to grow and take on a big challenge is another example of the prevailing philosophy of 'shared ownership' at the Dome.

None of the contractors working on the Dome had any problem accepting the deadline, but mistakes happen and people can fall behind through no fault of their own. In such cases — of which there were far fewer on the Dome than on many other smaller projects — David Trench's essentially pragmatic response was to make the best of potentially bad situations: 'Having signed a fairly draconian contract, I put it in a drawer and don't use it. The contract gives me the upper hand, but you shouldn't invoke the contract if it isn't in your interest.'

The Dome had to be built and it had to be built on time. If a legitimate claim was likely to be made, in other words, if it was inevitable that the client was going to bear an additional cost, maximum value

might as well be extracted from it. Where trade contractors got into difficulties, or where they fell behind and no one was to blame, he negotiated acceleration contracts or 'wrap-up deals' that essentially bought out the potential claim and gave the contractor a chance to rectify the problem. This represented 'value for money' in its fullest sense and contributed to positive site relations.

One such potential disaster occurred just a week before one of the core service buildings — Core 7, which housed the visitor preview centre — was due to be opened. The date in question was 300 days before the new millennium, one of the highly visible milestones that have punctuated the project. A VIP reception was planned in the visitor centre, where one of the project's major sponsors, Ford, would be announced. Then the ceiling fell in. David Trench describes the strategy in action: 'We had a real setback when the acoustic spray which is water-based seeped through the plasterboard which then loosened its nails and the whole lot fell on the floor. And it's a huge ceiling. The trade contractor was sitting there realizing he was going to go broke. I could have pulled the contract out and said it was the contractor's problem and he would have gone broke. But it doesn't give me my core building. I calculated the loss was £75,000. So I said to the contractor, if he could keep to the date, and this was only a week away, which meant working night and day, I'd pay £100,000 – and you know they did. Nobody believed they could do it. They took the thing and ran for it. And we opened the core on the date.'

On the design side, mistakes and setbacks also required compromise. But true compromise, which would keep the spirit of the project intact, depended on knowing what each other's real priorities were, where mistakes could be lived with and where they absolutely had to be put right. 'We're extremely pleased at how we have managed to build up a relationship with Richard Rogers Partnership and Buro Happold,' says Bernard Ainsworth. 'They are willing to share and to compromise at times. They haven't sat on their high horse.'

An innovative programme, developed by David Scott, offered a unique way of controlling the productivity of the multiple contractors on site. Each Monday a report was published that measured every contractor's production in man hours against projected targets. This allowed management to spot where potential areas of difficulty might develop. David Trench's daily site tour was an equally direct way of checking the pulse of the project: 'You have to check down below if you really want to know what's going on,' he says. Unsurprisingly, Bernard Ainsworth is another advocate of this type of informal information gathering, 'walking about, asking questions and reading the post'.

The planning process

There was, however, another aspect to building the Dome where very little could be streamlined. The Dome represented a hugely complicated planning process with permissions that had to be sought and gained from a wide variety of official bodies. In the initial planning application, as well as the plans for the Dome itself, about thirty other ancillary structures or features of the site as a whole were itemized, ranging from a shelter for coach drivers to a ticket booth for the pier. In many cases, this was inspired guesswork: an indication of just how inspired those predictions were can be gauged from the fact that only three major new permissions have subsequently had to be sought – for Skyscape ('Baby Dome'), the treatment of the piazza area and the Thames Water recycling building.

During the course of obtaining detailed permissions, a process that ran in parallel with a certain degree of design fluidity, the complexities multiplied. Any work near the river had to be cleared with Port of London Authority and the Environment Agency. Siteworks that involved digging or penetrating layers of contaminated ground had to comply with an enormous number of health and safety regulations. Method statements for such works had to be approved by environmental health officers. Transport strategies had to be submitted for approval, along with details of colour, lighting, landscaping, right down to species of tree.

Then there were the sixty planning conditions attached to the original permission that had to be discharged at the right time, otherwise the scheme would be in breach of its permission, all of which had to be cross-checked with English Partnerships and the conditions they in turn had to discharge on the masterplan regarding servicing, roads and landscaping. As soon as one set of conditions was discharged, the project accumulated new ones, as part of the process of gaining detailed permissions in each area. At the same time there were tortuous legal negotiations specifying the precise nature of the Section 106 Agreement with Greenwich, a contract detailing the 'planning gain' to the borough.

By far the most complex aspect of this process arose from dealings with the Highways Agency, who not only had their own conditions relating to the Blackwall Tunnel and its ventilation shaft, but had also earmarked a number of potential routes and future river crossings, routes which criss-crossed the map of the peninsula like a hatching of fine lines. Loading on the tunnel had to be measured and these measurements independently audited; computer analyses had to be undertaken of the airflow around the vent shaft and similarly checked. Tackling this entire bureaucratic hydra involved fortnightly meetings with planning officers and various officials, not to mention a mountain of paperwork. And as more people joined the project, constant updating was required to keep everyone in the picture.

Siteworks

A timetable of construction milestones had been built into the original programme prepared in the autumn of 1996. Although in detail some of these had subsequently been changed, the essentials remained the same. For purely practical purposes, hitting these marks was crucial if the Dome were to be ready on time. Psychologically, ticking off the milestones generated a powerful momentum for those working long hours to see the project through. Making these milestones highly visible and meeting the dates in public upped the ante considerably. 'The first target date, putting the first mast up, was a big milestone in my mind,' says Bernard Ainsworth. 'We set this date in the programme at the end of '96 and here was the mast going up on the date we'd set a year earlier. This setting of dates, making them very visible, was an important way of coping with the deadline.'

> *I'm a stickler for meeting dates. We've had 30 dates and we've met them all except two.*
>
> David Trench, NMEC

Achieving the dates was a total team effort, and it was key individuals such as Rolv Kristiansen who galvanized everyone on site to recognize them and take responsibility for them. His larger-than-life presence, sense of connection with the workers and thorough understanding of the site conditions helped immeasurably in the constant battle to deliver on time.

Hitting these milestones demanded coherent planning to make sure that conflicts did not arise between work carried out on behalf of English Partnerships as part of the masterplan development, and work carried out on the Dome. The overall strategy was to work from north to south down the peninsula, with work on the Dome following in the wake of English Partnerships work. At the same time, London Underground was still busy constructing the North Greenwich station which falls within the exhibition site area. Getting hold of the area where the Dome would be constructed called for complicated choreography. Once the structure was going up and construction works inside the Dome were under way, a further complication arose in ensuring that no work was ever carried out directly above ongoing works on the ground.

Decontamination

Preliminary remediation work was carried out on the site by British Gas, a process which began in the early summer of 1996. Under law, British Gas were obliged to remove all the known 'black spots' before the site

could be sold on. In practice, this included completely removing a large tar tank under what is now the Meridian Quarter, a tank which had broken and which, there was evidence to suggest, was leaking tar into the Blackwall Tunnel. Some of the remediation work also involved a massive 'water-washing' process, flushing out toxic wastes by pushing water into the ground through recharge wells. The aim was to remove all sources of ongoing problems, including contaminants which were 'mobile' and could potentially come in contact with the ground water and hence with the Thames. A site levelling process was also involved. Secondary remediation was subsequently carried out by English Partnerships, once the site had been sold. Nuttalls were the contractors engaged for these works.

The cleanup procedure was never envisaged as a removal of all contaminants. When it comes to dealing with pollution on this scale, the best environmental practice dictates that, instead of clearing away absolutely every trace of poisoned material and simply dumping it somewhere else – on someone else's doorstep, as it were – the answer is to remove as much as possible of the most hazardous materials and to cap the rest with a top level of clean ground. For the outside areas of the Dome, this layer is a metre deep. Within the Dome area itself, there is an additional barrier, a membrane below the ground-floor slab, serving to prevent gases from reaching the surface. This membrane alone cost £1 million.

Piling, groundworks and foundations

Among the first people to feel the hot breath of the approaching deadline on their necks were the engineers responsible for coming up with a way of founding the structure on the poor ground of the Greenwich site. British Gas, who still owned the land at the beginning of 1996, had employed W. S. Atkins to carry out the statutory site remediation. A consequence of the selection of Greenwich as the millennium site was that Buro Happold, as the consulting engineers for the entire project, effectively had to duplicate some of the investigation work that had already been carried out and to carry out these investigations while remediation work was under way. Digging holes in

As a diagram showing the typical ground sequence of the exhibition site reveals, the top layer of soil was heavily contaminated, which added to the difficulty of the groundworks *(right)*. Special decontamination procedures *(above left)* had to be followed for procedures which involved penetrating this layer *(left)*.

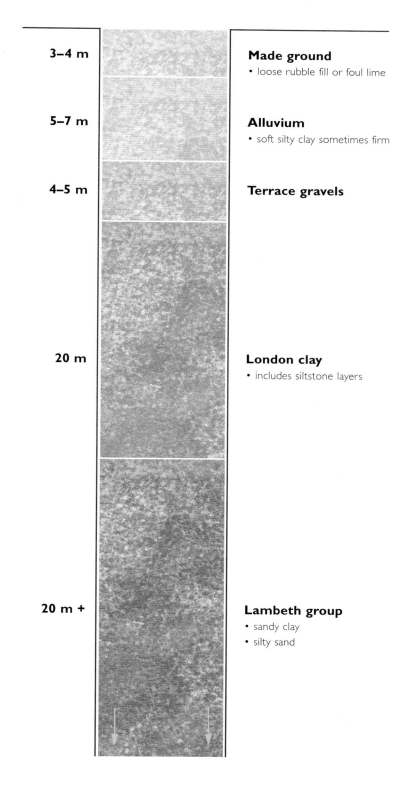

3–4 m

Made ground
• loose rubble fill or foul lime

5–7 m

Alluvium
• soft silty clay sometimes firm

4–5 m

Terrace gravels

20 m

London clay
• includes siltstone layers

20 m +

Lambeth group
• sandy clay
• silty sand

poisoned ground, while other contractors carried out their own difficult procedures on the same site, raised interesting contractual and operational issues.

Investigations, the results of which were not available until January 1997 after the scheme had gone in for planning, proved that the ground conditions were less promising than had first been imagined. The top layer of soil comprised some four metres of 'made' material, which was heavily contaminated. Directly underneath was a 6-metre-deep layer of the original marshland soils including soft clays, which acted as a barrier to the contamination spreading downwards. Under that was a five-metre layer of terrace gravels, which provided a water source, albeit one of poor quality. It was essential that no technique should be used in creating the foundations that would spread the contamination from the surface down through the alluvium into the gravels, and hence into the water supply. Below the gravels was a twenty-metre-deep layer of firm London clay.

A study of aerial photographs and old plans had indicated that there were also substantial obstructions below ground, including foundations of structures that had by now been demolished. These obstructions – metre-thick layers of concrete in places – would be difficult and expensive to break up. Part of the design jigsaw was to work out if there was any way in which they could be effectively reused.

From the outset it was clear that fairly substantial works would be necessary to take the load of the Dome down into the firm stratum of the gravels, and this meant piling. The uncertain nature of the Dome's contents posed another difficulty. Evaluations were done to see if raft or pad foundations would be sufficient for the proposed internal structures, simple foundations that essentially consist of concrete resting on the ground or extending only a small way under the surface. In many ways this might well have been a feasible solution were it not for an unpleasant discovery. One of the nastier by-products of producing town gas is foul lime. At the Greenwich works, once the gas had been passed through lime to cleanse it of impurities, the foul lime which resulted had just been dumped on the site. The foul lime was up to four metres deep in places across the area of the Dome. The presence of this extremely soft polluted material effectively ruled out the pad foundation option. Foundation settlements of up to 50mm could have been tolerated, but the foul lime meant that settlement of 300mm or more could well have been expected.

'We were pushing towards a solution that was more permanent, because whatever happened above ground, you were going to end up with a more permanent below-ground solution,' says Peter Scott of Buro Happold. 'At the same time, there was the other part of the equation, which was that they hadn't decided what they were going to

At the peak of activity, fourteen piling rigs were simultaneously working on site.

Driven cast *in situ* piling was the method used to create most of the 8,000 piles over the site area, but on either side of the shaft of the Blackwall Tunnel, continuous flight augur piles, which cause less vibration and can go deeper, were used instead *(far left)*.

put in the Dome. In terms of design, we were trying to optimize what we were doing and make it economical, but that had to be offset against the fact that we were not quite certain what was going to put where.'

Yet another problem was the presence, below the Dome and in the stratum of London clay, of the southbound Blackwall Tunnel. This critical underground structure had enormous implications for the design of the foundations. There were concerns about vibration affecting the lighting and internal features of the tunnel and about the loading on the tunnel itself. As two of the Dome's huge masts were to be situated directly above the tunnel and its surrounding exclusion zone, a foundation solution was required which would somehow take the load off the top of the tunnel and down the sides.

The design solution was to use continuous flight augur piles, bored through the gravels and down into the London clay on either side of the tunnel shaft, with huge reinforced concrete beams between the piles forming a bridge over the top. These piles, formed by drilling what resembles a huge corkscrew into the ground, and then pumping concrete down a tube in the middle as the corkscrew is withdrawn, can go deeper than other piles and can be of a larger diameter, which means that they have a higher capacity. They also cause less vibration, which meant they could be put in closer to the tunnel. The masts on their pyramid bases would therefore rest on the underground beams between the piles, with the piles in turn transferring this load down the sides of the tunnel deep into the clay.

Elsewhere, it was clear that the load would have to be taken down into the gravels. Different methods were evaluated in terms of time and cost, from vibratory techniques which have the virtue of being very fast but which might not have been sufficiently powerful to break up some of the underground obstructions, to driven cast *in situ* piling, which consists of driving a steel tube down into the ground, and then filling with concrete as the tube is withdrawn. The possibility was also investigated of using elements of the large buried structures as part-foundations.

After more than twelve months of preliminary investigation, analysis and trial works, the engineers finally concluded that the solution was to pile the whole site in a regular grid of driven cast *in situ* piles at three-metre centres, with continuous flight augur piles along the tunnel shaft. Given the open-ended nature of the project, it was the only sensible option. Flexibility, the defining characteristic of the Dome itself, was to begin right from below the ground.

'There is no point putting piles in or using existing piles if they are not in the right place,' says Peter Scott. 'On the one hand, it's cheaper to put the buildings where the piles are, especially when you don't know what all the buildings are going to be, but the whole process must be

driven by what you are trying to achieve. We concluded that the only way you could go ahead was to put in some form of regular grid. The buildings could not be determined by what was already in the ground.'

The importance of the Dome's first milestone, the completion of the piling works, could not be underestimated. How long would it take to drive the thousands of piles into the ground? The contract to carry out the piling was won by Keller Ground Engineering of Coventry. An example of the evolving nature of the design in relation to the timescale was that Keller was appointed on the basis of driving 5,000 piles in a thirteen-week period. The contract was completed on time, but by then Keller had successfully driven nearly 8,000 piles. The operation began on 23 June 1996, four days after the government announced the go-ahead. The 1,000th pile was driven into the ground by the Minister for London, Nick Raynsford, on 17 July in what was a more meaningful photo-opportunity than most. At the peak of activity, fourteen piling rigs were working simultaneously on site. Keller subsequently won the contract to construct the ground anchors.

> **All the work we do, no one ever sees any of it.**
> Colin Holdsworth, Joint Venture

A factor in the eventual selection of driven cast *in situ* piles was that they would not bring up contaminated matter from below ground. The continuous flight augur piles round the tunnel shaft were a different matter and a strategy had to be approved and agreed whereby the waste brought up from deep under the ground by this method would be disposed of and carried off the site. Similarly, ongoing monitoring had to be carried out to prove that the vibration from the piling works near the tunnel was not exceeding agreed limits.

The regular grid of piling designed by the engineers as a response to the considerable early unknowns of the project largely fitted the bill. But, as time went by, additional piling had to be carried out in areas where the grid did not match the evolving design. To avoid having to put in too many additional piles outside the Dome, preloading was carried out over areas where there was foul lime and where settlement was likely to be greatest. This involved laying an additional stratum of earth on top to stabilize the ground.

After the piling was complete, foundation work was carried out by John Doyle Construction, led by Alan Green, and O'Rourke Civil Engineering, led by Neil Henderson. This work included the construction of site drainage, service trenches, the ground-floor slab, bases for the Dome's masts, and the massive concrete ring beam that runs round the circumference of the Dome and resists the inwards pull of the structure. Eight metres wide, half a metre thick and a kilometre long, the ring beam represents some 5,000 cubic metres of reinforced concrete.

Nick Raynsford, Minister for London, drives the 1,000th pile into the Dome site *(far left)*. Workers engaged in constructing the foundations *(far left, below)*.

The 24 concrete anchor blocks positioned round the perimeter of the Dome resist the upwards pull of the radial cables, shown here under construction *(left)* and complete *(below)*. The foundations of each anchor extend over 24m into the ground.

The twelve steel masts

The yellow steel masts, soaring 100 metres into the air like the points of a giant crown, are the most spectacular feature of the Dome. The necessary preliminary stage of the siteworks may have been a real achievement, but the lifting of the masts represented the first visible evidence of progress. The first mast was erected on 13 October 1997. Yet months before, at the time of the government review, the masts had already been fabricated and were lying in the steel contractor's yard. Months before that, development work had been carried out by the engineers and contractors to finalize details of construction.

Fabrication

After a four-month tender period, in April 1997 Watson Steel of Bolton won the contract to supply both the masts and the cabling, and to erect the Dome. They had a 52-week programme to detail and fabricate the structural steelwork, procure the cables and carry out the erection. During the development period, a number of refinements were made to the design and some cost-saving measures were agreed.

Given that each mast weighs 95 tonnes and is 100 metres long, the intention had always been to manufacture the masts in sections and assemble them on site. As Joe Locke of Watson Steel explains: 'One of the most important modifications at development stage was to reduce the overall diameter of the masts to enable the sections to be transported by conventional road trailers.' Larger forms of transport would have required excessive notification periods because of potential traffic disruption. With the outcome of the project still uncertain, it was essential to be able to move the masts quickly from the factory to the site as soon as the go-ahead was given. Reducing the overall diameter meant than some of the longitudinal tubes that comprise each mast had to be increased in thickness. The length of each of the six sections was 15 metres; tubes could be obtained from the rolling mills in these lengths, which meant there was no need to join them in the factory.

Other design refinements concerned the detailing of the mastheads to allow access through the centre, and the introduction of platforms and ladders, features which would assist in the construction process. The base of the masts was also redesigned to provide more give at the point at which the masts connect to their pyramid bases.

Watson Steel then had the task of turning the engineer's drawings into 'shop' drawings, showing the cutting and holing dimensions of all the plates and the welding and connection details. Before each part could be manufactured, the shop drawings went back to the architects and engineers for their approval.

Watson Steel of Bolton won the contract to construct the Dome's 12 masts, to supply the cabling and to erect the structure. Each mast was manufactured in sections *(far left)* to simplify the transport arrangements. Completed sections were stored in Watson Steel's yard *(left)*, but final assembly was to take place on site. The fabrication of the steelwork called for pinpoint accuracy to make sure every element fitted together. The masts were manufactured to such a degree of precision that every section proved to be interchangeable. Some of the many steel fabrications required to connect the cables to the masts *(overleaf)*.

All the joints in the masts were fully welded, a decision based on aesthetics as much as economy. But with each mast having to be finally assembled and welded on site from six individual sections, and some of the masts being manufactured in Bolton and some in Bristol, there was an acute need for pinpoint accuracy. Watson Steel produced sets of matching templates to guarantee this perfect fit. The tolerance they achieved was tiny, only 1mm each way in the diameter of the tubes. The level of care that went into the fabrication was triumphantly demonstrated when site assembly began in July 1997. All the mast sections slotted together perfectly; so perfectly, in fact, the sections also proved to be interchangeable.

Once they had been transported down the motorway and had arrived on site, the mast sections were laid out horizontally on special supports and welded together. Covers were set up to protect the joints from rain and 480 welds were completed in seven weeks without a single repair being necessary. While the masts were down on the ground, the huge extractor fans that would control the Dome's ventilation were also installed, as well as some temporary winching gear that would be used to lift the cable net from the top of each mast. The 12 four-legged pyramid bases were assembled on site at the same time, stood on their concrete bases and bolted in position.

Lifting the masts

One of the most complicated and potentially risky parts of the whole procedure then began: lifting the masts. As Paul Westbury says: 'It's one thing to analyse how the mast is going to behave when it's up there, but getting it there can overstress it or produce stresses that are very different from the final conditions.' At this intermediate stage, when the masts were being manoeuvred into place, they would be at their most vulnerable. Buro Happold had produced an outline method statement for lifting the masts in their tender documentation, whereby the masts would have been lifted with the hangar cables attached to them and there would have been a temporary central tower to guy the masts using the permanent cables. Watson Steel, however, preferred to assemble the cable net on the ground and then hoist it to the mast tops with the hangar cables, a method that had certain design implications for the mast tops and for the way the masts would be lifted.

After further refinements and testing with the Tensyl program, it was decided to hold each mast in place before the cable net was lifted by using four stays: two permanent backstays going to the anchor blocks

> *The Dome has a very positive geometric form. One of its features is that all the masts point towards the theoretical centre of the sphere. Any two masts will always line up and that has a subconscious impact on people.*
>
> Ian Liddell, Buro Happold

and two temporary forestays going to the centre of the Dome area. Design checks had shown that it would be necessary to lift the mast at four different positions to prevent the failure of the welded joints.

The day the first mast went up, a large crowd of VIPs and press representatives gathered on site to see one of the largest cranes in Europe raise 95 tonnes of steelwork into the air. A smaller crane controlled the bottom of the mast and gingerly manoeuvred it into position on its pyramid base. It was a heart-stopping moment. Then a cradle took three trained abseilers (two to lift the cables and one 'in case of incident') up to the platform on top of the mast in order to winch in the stays and connect them in position. Hours later, when the stays had been finally tensioned, the mast stood free of the crane, at precisely the correct angle of 17 degrees to the vertical. The operation had worked, and it would be successfully completed eleven more times over the following sixteen days. As Niels Cross, Buro Happold's site engineer, says, 'The great thing about the Dome is that because everything repeats twelve times, you learn the first time round and by the end you're doing it so much quicker.'

The original plan was for the masts to be left in the standard industrial finish, the engineering or industrial grey of the micaceous iron oxide coating, a finish familiar on bridges and similar structures. This was, of course, the cheap answer. 'Our firm enjoys colour immensely,' says Mike Davies, 'and Richard [Rogers] was saying, "Couldn't we have a really bright colour instead?" We had a late emergency meeting with Jennie and suggested that the masts should be painted the colour of Van Gogh cornfields – we're always using painting analogies for buildings. It's a wonderful colour, the colour of summer and of heat.' It cost more, but the architects won the day, and the masts were painted 'Van Gogh cornfield yellow' prior to assembly.

The bright yellow mast sections were brought to the site on large road trailers. Each one is 15 metres long *(right)*. Once on site, the sections were laid out on specially constructed supports for final welding together *(overleaf)*.

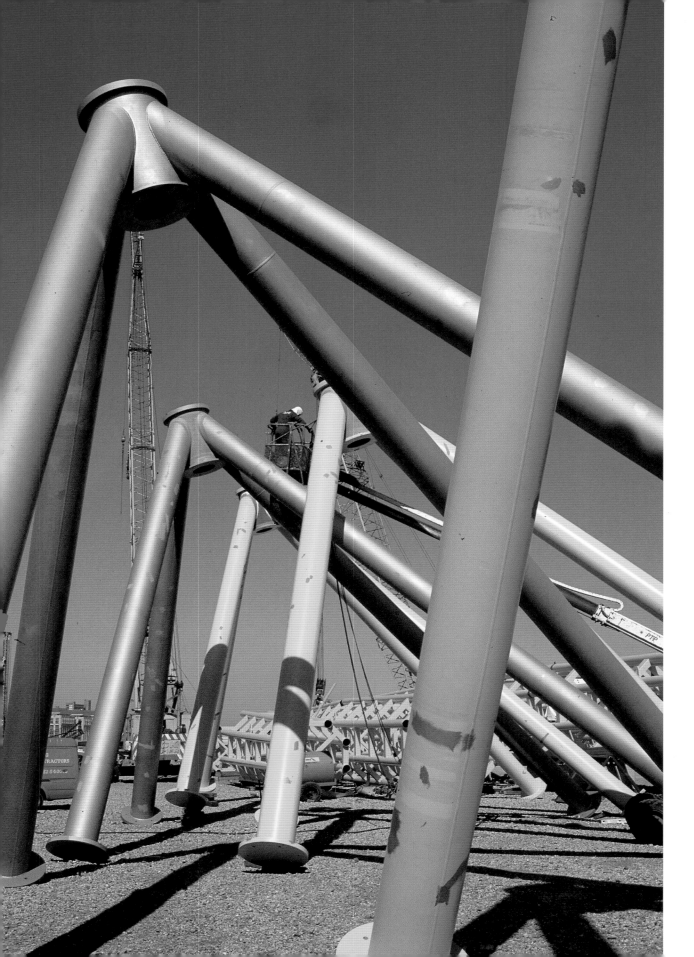

A series of flanges or lugs positioned at each end of the masts serve as connection points for the cabling. Part of the process of design development was to ensure that these connections – some of which would have to be made 100 metres off the ground – could be executed in a straightforward fashion and that none of the cables would conflict *(far left)*. While the masts were being assembled, their pyramid bases were also constructed on site. These four-legged steel bases are based around the 'redundancy principle'. If one of the four legs were to fail, the mast would still be stable *(left)*.

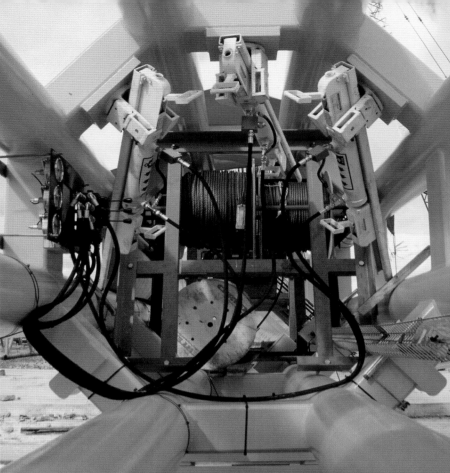

The Dome's masts, from which the cable network is suspended, are major structural elements. But once erected they were also to play a vital role in the construction process. The interior of the mast sections were fitted with access ladders *(left, below)* to enable workers to reach the top where the cable connections would be made *(far left, above)*. While the masts were still on the ground, temporary winching gear was installed so that the cables could be hoisted into position *(left, above)*. Each mast is also fitted with an extractor fan to aid the Dome's ventilation *(far left, below and above)*. Finally, workers secured each mast to the crane that would lift it into position *(right)*.

Prior to lifting, the fully assembled masts were laid out in their clockface positions *(above)*. The first mast was lifted on 13 October 1997. One of the largest cranes in Europe was used for the monumental task of lifting the 95 tonnes of steelwork into the air, a crane so huge that it had taken 24 lorries to bring it to the site. A smaller crane was also necessary to manoeuvre the mast into position. While the masts were being lifted they were at their most vulnerable – design checks showed that they had to be lifted in four different positions to prevent their welded joints from failing.

Before the cable net was erected, the masts were held in place by four cables. Two of these cables were permanent backstays secured at the anchor blocks *(below centre)*. The other two cables were temporary forestays which were secured at the centre of the Dome area *(below)*.

Practice makes perfect. The Dome's circularity means that the entire construction process has been highly repetitive. Lifting the first mast was a major milestone, but as the tenth, eleventh and twelfth masts went up, the process went with increasing smoothness and speed *(left)*. In the end, it took just over two weeks for all twelve masts to be lifted and guyed into their correct positions.

The cable net

The articulation of the cable net, the many points of connection between lengths of cable and between the cables and the masts, makes the structure of the Dome read very finely, even though the elements — thick cabling and large pieces of metal assembly — are far from delicate.

Yet appearances are not entirely deceptive. When it came for the cable net to be installed, this fineness was matched by an equal demand for precision, tiny tolerances of millimetres which were required for the structure to work. It was one of the biggest assembly kits in history.

While the connection points provide a human scale, a reference that gives the structure a certain tactility, the details of the fixings are an honest expression of the engineering function they are performing: they are not preciously designed, but have a utilitarian, industrial aesthetic. Equally important, most of these connections were made by hand, with a large proportion of this physical work being done by abseilers, suspended like spiders underneath the web of the net.

The aeronauts of the construction team, the abseilers from specialist rope-access firm CAN, captured everyone's imagination. In an odd sort of way, their manoeuvrings high above the ground, dangling from masts or suspended from the cable net, prefigured the acrobatics that would later form the heart of the Dome's central show. From the guying of the masts to making the cable connections and clamping the fabric panels in place, they were an ever-present feature of the site until the final topping out ceremony when the big roof was complete.

Firms like CAN tackle any job that requires basic rope skills and heights to be scaled: drilling rock faces, working on suspension bridges and oil rigs, or even cleaning skyscraper windows. Many of CAN's abseilers, who included climbers, cavers and potholers, were in the enviable position of being able to do what they loved all day and get paid for it. Time off generally meant more of the same. 'They used to work twelve days on and two days off,' says Peter Miller of Watson Steel, 'and often on those two days off they would go away mountaineering. They were brilliant, absolutely brilliant.'

> *It's about network rather than monumentality. When the Dome was up as a cable structure, which is the real structure, it looked like a gossamer spider's web, a very minimalist structure. The fabric cover is 1mm thick, that's all. If you take the skin off, the whole thing disappears, there's just a bit of framework left.*
>
> **Mike Davies, Richard Rogers Partnership**

Assembly

The cable-net assembly began, however, more prosaically on the ground. The idea was to carry out as much work as possible before lifting the assembly in the air, and to lift the assembly in as large sections as possible. This was not only easier, it also minimized the risk for those who would be working at a high level.

Bridon International of Doncaster, subcontracted by Watson Steel, manufactured the cables for the Dome. The cables had to be prestressed in a special track 750 metres long before being cut to length *(left)*.

The cables themselves had been manufactured to a very close tolerance, by Bridon International of Doncaster, subcontracted by Watson Steel. The cables, drawn from wires and galvanized, were pre-stressed in a special prestressing bed – a track 750 metres long – and then cut to length. In other words, they were pulled to the load under which they would subsequently perform and then cut. This was not a simple question of measuring and marking off: if the loading was wrong, the length would also be wrong.

Simon Barlow of Watson Steel explains: 'Once the cables arrived on site, the plan was to assemble and lift up the central ring first [known as "circ 1"], then to lift the remaining six circumferential cables in pairs: circ 2 and 3; circ 4 and 5; circ 6 and 7.' The radial cables comprise a series of discrete lengths running between node points; each complete radial, from the central ring to the perimeter edge, is made up of six individual lengths. While the cables were still on the ground, the radials between each pair of circumferential cables were connected.

Lifting the circumferentials in pairs, however, did mean that some of the radials – those running between each connected pair of circumferentials – were going to have to be connected in the air. While the cables were still on the ground, these radials were also attached, with their free ends looped off.

Lifting the net

The central ring was hoisted into the air from the mastheads using the twelve permanent forestay cables, each attached to a temporary pulling cable. Twelve temporary tie-down cables were then put in place, running from the central ring down to the ground, so that the temporary forestays, which had been holding the masts in position since they were erected, could be removed. (These forestays would have been in the way when the remainder of the nets were lifted.)

Lifting each subsequent pair of circumferential cables, with their connecting radials, was achieved in the same way, by simultaneously pulling on temporary extension cables attached to the permanent hangars. There were three pull jacks at the top of each mast, controlled by a single operator, working to an agreed signal transmitted by radio from the foreman in charge. Because the nets were still flexible, there could be a differential of about one metre between the levels of the individual lifting points, a margin which was judged by eye. It was slow and steady progress: the nets were raised at a rate of about 10 metres per hour. All of the lifting equipment had been specially designed and had been subjected to a full working trial at Bolton in the autumn of 1997, which had resulted in some improvements being made. After the work at the mastheads was completed, it would all be removed and lowered to the ground.

Once each pair of circumferential cables was at its full height, and the ends of the hangar cables were within reach of the mastheads, these permanent cables could then be connected. Twelve pairs of abseilers, one pair for each mast, climbed through the tops of the masts and abseiled down the outside to the connection points to tackle this difficult procedure. Working 100 metres above the ground in freezing winter temperatures, the abseilers installed 276 connecting pins over a period of months between late 1997 and early 1998 – a dizzying feat of aerial dexterity.

Now that all the cable rings were up in the air, the looped-off radials could be also be connected to their circumferentials – work again carried out by the abseilers using lightweight winching equipment. At the edge the radials were connected to the scalloped boundary cables. When the entire cable net was up and connected, it sagged baggily in the air. The next stage would be to tension it.

Tensioning the net

Each of the paired 72 radial cables was tensioned at its perimeter mast. At the top of each mast was a lug with a hole in it. At the end of each radial was a cable plate with a central hole. Between the two was a hydraulic tension jack with a 55-tonne capacity. As the jack drew the two elements together, bottle screws were wound up to hold everything in position. The tensioning, which had to result in a final cable load of 40 tonnes, was done in four stages: 20 per cent, 80 per cent, 95 per cent, then 100 per cent, with teams working on opposite sides and moving round the Dome.

The critical part of the process was surveying the position of the perimeter masts and adjusting everything so that the tops of the masts ended up in their correct positions. This called for great precision. In theory, if the positioning was properly controlled, then the structure should have all the right tensions. At the same time, the tensions were also monitored using the hydraulic jacks. 'Generally,' says Glyn Trippick, 'we managed to get all the masts to within plus or minus 25mm of their nominal position. When we got that position, all our tensions in our radial cables were within 10 per cent of what we had predicted.' With some understatement he adds: 'We were pleased that the computers got it right and the erection team got it right. In fact, Watson Steel said they would have loved to have done it all over again. Because they learned so much, they said they could have done it in half the time.'

> *The whole idea of a structure just with tensioned cables and nothing else to control the fabric is new.*
>
> Ian Liddell, Buro Happold

As the great masts went up, one of the biggest assembly kits in history – the individual lengths of cables and their many connections – was simultaneously being laid out on the ground. The aim was to make as many of the cable connections as possible before the net was lifted, so as little work as possible was required high up in the air.

The central ring, or 'circ 1', was the first part of the cable net to be lifted into the air *(above right)*. Each of the 72 lines of radial cables starts from this central ring – it literally holds the whole roof together, carrying a massive load of 700 tonnes. Early on, it was planned for the central ring to be a single steel fabrication, but this was changed for the safer option of a cable ring, composed of 12 cables, two rows of six one above the other, clamped together. A conical central truss forms the hub of the ring *(above)*. Slowly and steadily, the first cable ring was hoisted into the air from the mastheads *(overleaf)*.

Conditions can be bleak on the Greenwich peninsula, particularly in the winter months when the wind blows from the northeast – there is said to be little land higher than 100 metres between the site and the steppes of Russia. The freezing winter months of late 1997 and early 1998 saw work progress on the cable net *(above and left)*. After the central ring was lifted *(right)*, the remaining circumferential cables were lifted in pairs. The radials that would connect them together were attached on the ground and looped off *(above right)*.

The web takes shape. With the
central ring in place, together
with the next pair of connected
circumferential cables, the fine
network of the Dome's structure
was beginning to come together.
At this stage, the cabling had not
been tensioned, so the net hung
baggily in the air.

The Blackwall Tunnel vent structure, falling within the footprint of the Dome, is dwarfed by the masts towering 100 metres into the air.

The steel structure of a core service building goes up under the cable net *(above)* – organizing the site called for a complicated choreography of movement so that work was never taking place directly above construction on the ground. The 72 perimeter masts control the ends of the radial lines of cable. At the edge of the cable net there are special connections in the form of two large plates bolted together. These transfer the load of the radial cable to the large scallop or boundary cable through friction *(below)*. To achieve this, the plates had to be clamped together very tightly *(right)*.

The first cable ring was lifted into its final position 50 metres off the ground in mid-November 1997 *(above left)*. By January the network was almost complete *(below left)*; mid-February 1998 and the Dome's structure is finally in place, with the cable net fully tensioned to resist loads that are equivalent to 25 jumbo jets taking off at full thrust *(above and overleaf)*.

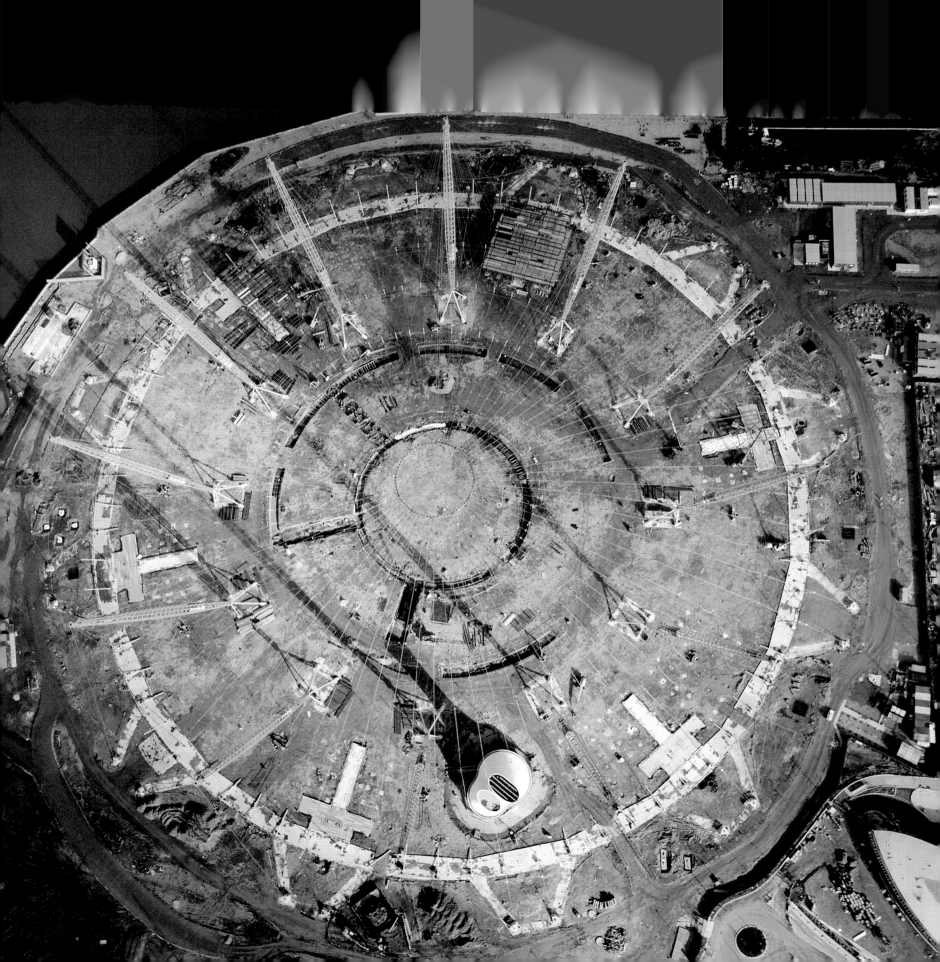

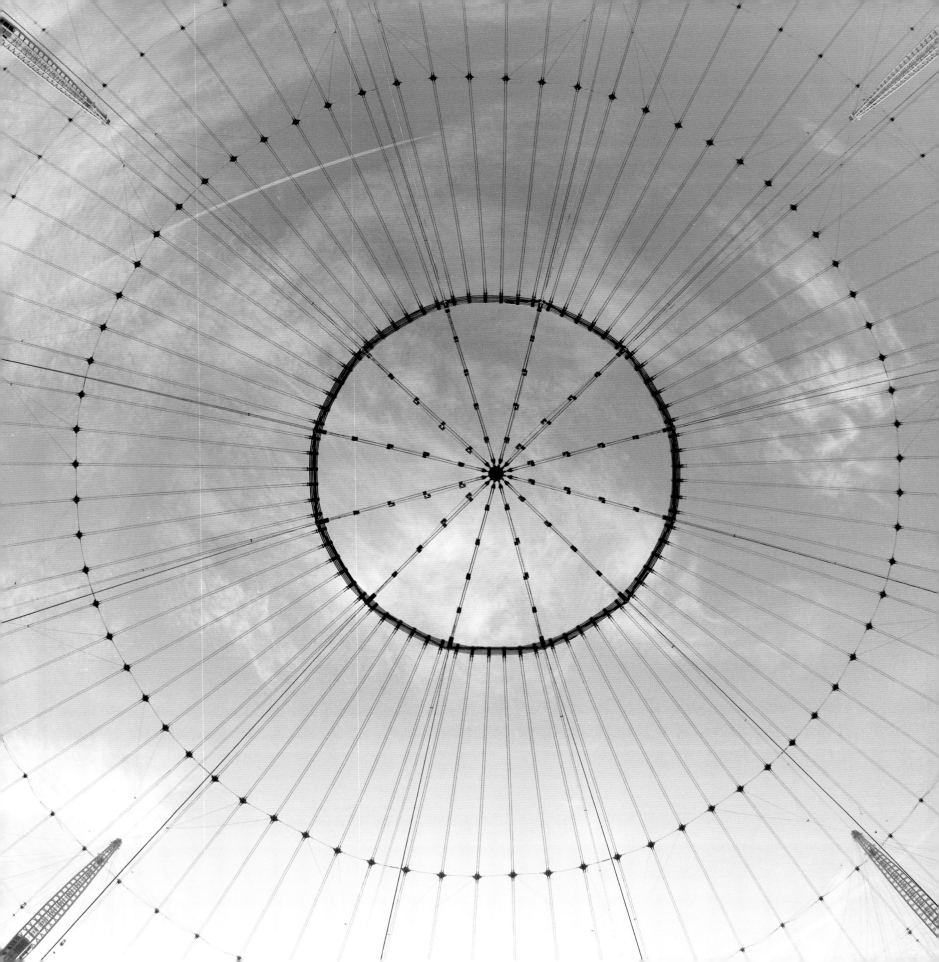

The roof

The Dome's canopy – 100,000 square metres or 25 acres of fabric cladding (double the size if the fabric lining is taken into account) – is the essential barrier to an inhospitable climate. Only when it was installed could construction work on the infrastructure and exhibits begin properly. The date when the structure would be weatherproof was consequently one of the most critical in the entire programme. As events turned out, it was also the date most at risk. The change in the choice of roof fabric, brought about by the new requirement that the Dome should have a longer life, wiped out three months of detailed design. The change in roof fabric meant all the fixing details would be different. Efforts to make up the lost time and keep to the original programme went on round the clock. 'There were a lot of late nights worked,' says Rolv Kristiansen. 'Until we had the roof up we couldn't really put too much other work on site, because we could never work below where we were working above.'

The change of roof fabric

Around the time that the tender documentation was being prepared for the steelworks, Buro Happold also began to consider the options for covering the big roof. The firm had worked on a project for a covered city in the Arctic, and research undertaken for that scheme had indicated that most people preferred the interiors of large covered areas to be naturally bright, which meant that roof coverings had to be translucent. If possible, the light spectrum should also be as close to daylight as possible: good colour rendering would be an important consideration for the designers of the Dome's content.

As well as providing a bright interior, the fabric covering had to be strong, durable and flame-resistant. Only two fabrics are suitable for this type of structure: polyester coated with PVC (polyvinylchloride), and glass fibre coated with PTFE (polytetrafluoroethylene, or Teflon). In the case of the polyester fabric, the PVC coating is designed to protect the fibres from ultraviolet radiation and to provide flame-proofing. In the case of the glass-fibre material, which is inherently fireproof, the Teflon coating protects the fibres from water damage. The PTFE-coated fabric has a lower translucency than the PVC-coated fabric, but it is less prone to discoloration and dirt retention. The other main differences between the two options concern price and longevity, with the PVC-coated polyester having a relatively short life, but being significantly cheaper and easier to detail, and the PTFE-coated glass fibre having a much longer life and costing considerably more. Structures clad in PTFE-coated glass fibre have been around for over a quarter of a century;

With the cable net completed, the next stage was to put on the Dome's fabric roof. At the same time, the central assembly of opening vents and fans had to be lifted to the top of the structure and installed. The only way of achieving this was to construct scaffolding in the middle and hoist the assembly up – the scaffolding would also provide access for the fabric installation.

the roof of the first such structure, in Florida, has shown no signs of degradation in nearly thirty years and there is every chance the material could last another couple of decades.

It was decided to explore both options. When the bids for the supply and erection of the roof fabric came in, the cheapest for the PVC-coated polyester option came from a German firm, Koch Hightex. 'The cheapest quote for the PTFE-coated glass fibre came from Birdair, an American company based in Buffalo, New York, with twenty years' experience in the use of the material to cover structures, including twelve stadiums of approximately half the size of the Dome,' says Roger Morehen, responsible for managing the procurement process. 'However, the price differential, at £8 million, was considerable.' At this time, before the government review in June 1997, the intention was still for the Dome to be a temporary structure and it was felt that the £8 million could be better spent on other aspects of the project as a whole. The PVC-coated polyester fabric was accordingly chosen. A letter of intent was issued to Koch Hightex in April 1997 and work started on the development of details.

The situation radically changed following the June 1997 review, when the new Labour government announced that one of the conditions on which the project should go ahead was that options should be kept open regarding the longer-term use of the Dome. This proviso completely changed the basis on which the fabric had been chosen.

The original tenders were reviewed again and it was decided that, given this new requirement for longevity, it would be better to opt for the better quality, longer-lasting material. As no extra funding would be forthcoming to make the change, the extra cost was met from contingency. Even taking into consideration the payments that would have to be made to Koch Hightex, Birdair still looked the cheapest option for the PTFE-coated fabric, so the arrangement with the German firm was terminated and a new contract was drawn up with Birdair. Several months of detailing the fabric patterning and attachments had been lost, time that could not be added on to the programme but would simply have to be made up by the designers.

The period of deliberation over the choice of roof fabric coincided with a particularly vociferous worldwide campaign mounted by Greenpeace against the use of PVC. Inevitably, the story blew up in the press. As Jennie Page remarks, 'Unfortunately in the well-known habit of the Dome, everything that happens turns into a major publicity story.'

Another Dome record-breaker – the largest free-standing scaffolding ever constructed provided a platform from which to position the central ventilation cap and also gave access to the workers fixing the fabric roof.

The client team at that time was very small, with only one person, Ross Cook, working in the press office trying to refute the wilder accusations about the Dome's so-called 'plastic roof'. Gregor Harvie, the project's 'technical troubleshooter', spent six months researching the subject and could not find any proven technical basis for what was being said against the PVC option, accusations that ranged from the possibility of 'toxic fumes' hovering over Greenwich, to the notion that the use of phthalates as plasticizers in the fabric's coating might get into the environment and act as an oestrogen mimic, causing fish, for example, to change sex. Such claims proved to rest on hotly contested evidence.

Timing, however, is all. When the PVC-coated fabric was subsequently dropped in favour of the longer-term PTFE solution, Greenpeace were able to claim a public relations triumph. But the damage had been done. After all the acres of press coverage devoted to the issue, the idea that the Dome was 'plastic' had lodged itself in the minds of the public, seemingly for good.

Putting on the fabric

The structure was up, its fine-spun elegance and delicate transparency belying the massive tensions holding it in place, tensions equivalent to 25 jumbo jets taking off at full thrust. With the cable net now stressed to the required shape, it was ready for the installation of the fabric covering. In the programme, 23 March 1998 was identified as the date for fabric installation to begin; it was a date, despite all the problems associated with the change in roof material, that was met.

The engineers had worked day and night to make up the time lost when the fabric was changed, detailing new connections to hold the fabric in place and designing the patterning of the fabric itself. Because the fabric panels were to be fitted between the cable net to dead lengths, the patterning of the fabric had to be extremely accurate. The basic geometry of the fabric patterning was modelled on computer by Buro Happold and converted into cutting patterns by the contractor Birdair. The fabric itself was manufactured by an American company, Chemical Fabrics Corporation.

At the same time, an erection procedure had to be worked out. The cladding would comprise 72 panels fitted between the radial cables, each panel made up of two lengths: that was 144 individual pieces, each about 75 metres long. While the glass-fibre fabric was only 1mm thick, the larger pieces would weigh over a tonne. There was also a central cap assembly to be fitted to the top of the roof, an assembly comprising 36 opening vents and 12 fans designed to aid the ventilation of the Dome. Baco, the British firm who won the contract for this central cap, considered various options for its installation, but came to the conclusion that the only way of tackling the problem was to put up a large free-standing scaffolding in the middle of the structure. 'It's the largest free-standing scaffolding ever erected,' says John Payne from Baco, who erected the scaffold. 'It's one thing that has gone in the *Guinness Book of Records.*' When the scaffolding was erected, a small crane was lifted to the top to lift up the individual units of the central cap assembly.

The hoist on the side of the scaffolding also provided Birdair with a useful means of access for lifting up men and equipment to carry out the fabric installation. The fabric was installed, however, not from the scaffolding, but from steel gantries hung from the cable net. Two sets of gantries, on opposing sides, were moved round to erect the panels. Three panels could be installed from each gantry position before the gantries needed to be moved. The panels themselves came crated to site, folded specially concertina-wise so that they opened in the correct way for the erection. They were lifted up to the gantry by crane and temporarily supported on cradles of ropes and belts slung between the radial cables before being unfurled and pulled out.

Buro Happold had to develop all the fabric fixing details. Working closely with Stan Kopaskie from Birdair they came up with a system using two-piece aluminium extrusion clamps. A 12mm cable ran through a cuff in the edge of the fabric panels, exposed at intervals by cutouts. The top piece of the aluminium clamp hooked over these edge cables, the bottom piece secured the radial cables and the whole assembly was bolted together. The clamps – 25,000 of them – were put onto the radial cables before the fabric was laid out. Once the fabric was in position, special pulling equipment was used to bring the edge cables onto the hooks and tension the fabric.

During all this time, because of the tight programme, work was also being carried out on the ground, constructing the core buildings that would house the Dome's servicing. The fabric installation had to be carefully planned so that at no time was work on the roof carried out directly above work on the ground. This continual movement of workers above and on the ground demanded the utmost coordination.

If connecting the cable net had resembled a high-wire act, the windy conditions on the peninsula meant that installing the fabric was at times more like tying down sails in a storm. As at sea, sudden gusts of wind were potentially more dangerous than a steady blow. When wind speeds topped 25mph, certain precautions had to be taken; over 35mph and work generally came to a halt. The upper panels of fabric weigh 700 kilogrammes, but the larger lower panels, which are twelve metres wide at the base, weigh 1,200 kilogrammes. Hauling each one into place took a team of fifteen men working with a crane and two winches. Hanging from the safety lines that criss-crossed the Dome, the abseilers used pre-stretched caving rope – in total 14 miles of it – rather than the usual abseiling or climbing rope, which is not designed to be used continuously.

THE ROOF   111

The change in the choice of fabric for the roof
meant that new fixing details had to be designed.
The fabric would be held in place by two-piece
aluminium clamps – 25,000 in total – each fixed to
the cable net by abseilers, dangling from the cable
network high above the ground.

While the scaffolding provided a means of access for those putting on the roof fabric, the panels that comprise the huge canopy of the Dome were actually installed from steel gantries hung under the cable net *(above and left)*. Each panel arrived on site specially folded so that it opened in the correct way *(below left)*. Three panels could be installed from each gantry position *(below and below right)*.

Not everything went according to plan. One day, during the installation of the fabric, an enormous judder ran through the whole structure, sending those working at the higher level scrambling for the safety of the central scaffolding. Something had slipped. At the edge of the cable net, there are special connections in the form of two large plates bolted together, which are designed to transfer the load of the radial cable to the large scallop or boundary cable through friction. To achieve this, these plates have to be clamped very tightly together, otherwise, with forces pulling in different directions, everything will move out of place. 'You need to put a large torque in the bolts, because if you don't, the thing will slide up,' says Glyn Trippick. 'And if it moves, it doesn't just move a little, it moves to the point where it's happiest and that's two metres away.' As it turned out, one of the clamps had only had been tightened to two-thirds of the final torque. 'In this type of situation you wonder whether you have got the calculations right and whether it will happen again. We checked the torque in all the bolts all the way round again and it was just that one.'

The Dome topped out on 22 June 1998, almost a year to the day after piling had started. The lace of the cable-net structure was finally covered with its pristine fabric skin. As the abseilers spiralled down from the roof in the topping out ceremony, watched by the Prime Minister and a battalion of press, it signalled a key milestone in the Dome's story.

> *When the abseilers came down from the roof in the topping out ceremony, I loved it. I absolutely loved it.*
>
> Jennie Page, NMEC

Sealing and weatherproofing

Each panel had a closure flap which was folded out to cover the cable lines. Once the panels were all attached, these flaps were temporarily

secured with stitching. Final sealing was done using an interlayer and an iron heated to 380 degrees Celsius. Waterproofing the node points also involved a great deal of work.

A distinctive feature of the Dome's exterior are the yellow caps that cover the top of the perimeter masts and the fixing points of the radial cables. The architects had always been keen to expose these critical parts of the structure and it was originally hoped that the masts could be capped with clear 'cockpit covers' made of polycarbonate. But the rigidity of these covers simply would not have provided enough movement and it was decided to cover the mast ends with fabric. As these covers had to be made of a different fabric (the glass-fibre fabric was not suitable) and hence would always weather differently, rather than opt for the same colour as the rest of the roof, the deliberate accent of bright yellow was chosen, signalling the presence of the perimeter masts on the outside of the structure.

Around the twelve main masts themselves, a closure system also had to be developed to keep the structure watertight. The fabric was fixed to an aluminium assembly attached to the stainless-steel ring round each masthead and the ring was covered with polycarbonate.

Enclosing the vent

The projected floor area of the Dome had to be large enough for an estimated 35,000 visitors a day to move comfortably around the exhibition. Given the layout of the site, the extent of this floor area meant that there was no option but for the Blackwall Tunnel vent to fall within the actual footprint of the Dome. There had never been any chance of repositioning: the vent was right in the middle, right in the way.

The vent, which comprises a large exhaust outlet and a smaller funnel which is the fresh air intake for the southbound tunnel, is a powerfully sculptural piece of industrial design with an essential role. It could not be entirely enclosed. Regulations stipulated that the smaller outlet had to remain in fresh air, which in turn meant that a large hole would have to be fashioned in the roof of the Dome. While it is relatively straightforward to design an enclosure to screen the vent from the interior of the Dome, the hole itself posed greater engineering difficulties. Removing such a large portion of the Dome's roof would slacken the tension in the fabric covering. The answer was to 'fool' the fabric into thinking that the hole was covered using a network of cable to replicate the forces that would have otherwise existed. Essentially a fabric with a very open weave, this network is comprised of 8-millimetre cables at 1-metre spacing.

The Dome's roof is made up of 144 individual panels – 72 in the upper ring and 72 in the lower.
As panels were unfurled to complete the upper ring, they provided a surface from which to work.
While the fabric is a mere 1mm thick, the larger panels in the lower section weigh over a tonne
and had to be hauled into place by a team of fifteen men working with a small crane and winches.

Over eighty abseilers from specialist rope-access firm CAN worked on the installation of the fabric covering, swarming over the creamy white surface of the roof or suspended from the cable net. As well as fixing the aluminium clamps to the cabling, and manoeuvring large unwieldy panels of fabric into position, they also had the task of securing the fabric to the cables and tensioning it. The windy conditions on the peninsula meant that installing the roof was at times rather like tying down sails in a storm. When wind speeds topped 35mph, work generally was called to a halt.

Although great strides had been made in the construction of the core service buildings, only when the Dome was fully covered could work properly begin inside on the exhibition areas. As the lower panels were installed one by one round the circumference, the date approached when the Dome would be a weatherproof structure. Inside, the roof is lined in a special fabric which is designed to absorb sound and prevent the build-up of condensation.

The vast scale of the Dome is tempered by a tactility that is visible in the many points of connection between fabric, cabling and masts, connections all made by hand. As a result, despite the advanced levels of technology required to analyse and design this complex structure, the Dome retains a certain human quality.

The topping out ceremony on 22 June 1998, when the big roof was complete, marked an important psychological milestone in the short history of the project. A year almost to the day after work first began on site, the entire structure of masts and cable net had been erected and the fabric covering installed. The Dome was on cost, on time and on track. The ceremony was attended by leading political figures, as well as the Dome's creators, among them Jennie Page *(centre left, top)*, Mike Davies and Richard Rogers *(centre left, bottom)*. Abseilers spiralled down from the roof to present a plaque to the Prime Minister Tony Blair, the Deputy Prime Minister John Prescott, the Secretary of State for Culture, Media and Sport Chris Smith and Minister without Portfolio Peter Mandelson, who hammered their initials into its surface to commemorate the event. Then it was back to the top of the roof, 50 metres off the ground, to fix the plaque in place.

The final task on the roof was to seal and weatherproof both the joins between fabric panels and round the tops of the masts. Each panel of fabric had a closure flap that was folded out over the cable lines; this was heat-sealed *(below)*. Round the masts, the fabric was attached to a steel ring that was covered with polycarbonate *(right)*. Round the perimeter, where the roof met the ground, polycarbonate walling was installed *(far right)*.

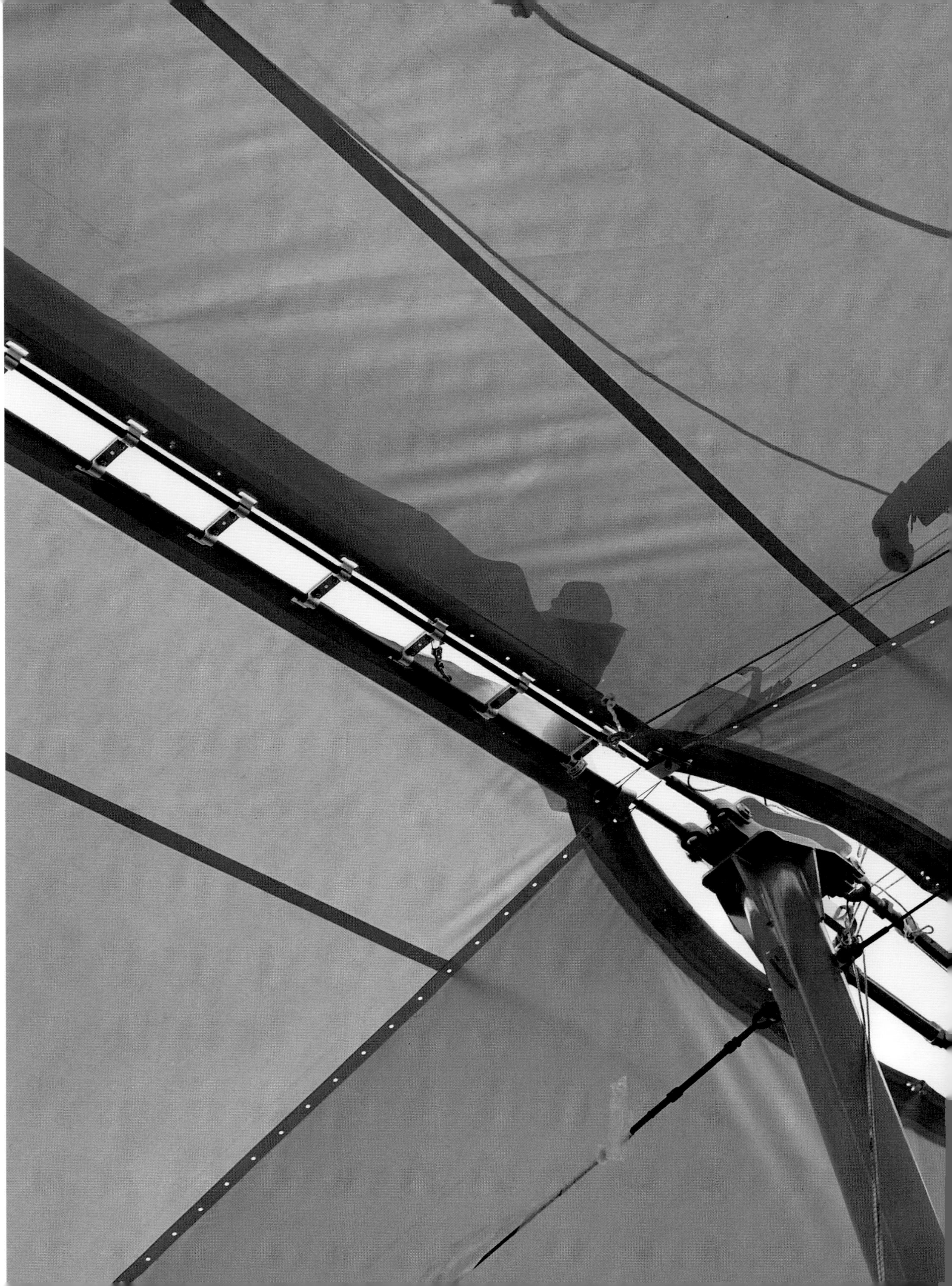

The perimeter mastheads are covered with bright yellow fabric caps to announce their presence on the exterior of the Dome.

The tight programme called for a high degree of coordination of activity on site.
Work begins preparing the outside areas round the Dome.

The Blackwall Tunnel vent, which falls within the Dome area, was subject to rigorous health and safety analysis. The vent had to remain accessible for maintenance purposes but tests had to be carried out to make sure that once enclosed, there would be no build-up of fumes that could either harm maintenance workers or escape into the Dome itself. Screening the vent from the interior of the Dome was straightforward *(below and below right)*. The necessary hole in the roof, however, was a different matter. The engineering solution was to fill the hole with a cable network which 'fooled' the roof fabric into thinking that the hole was not there *(right and far right)*.

Services

Like the Dome's structure, its servicing can be read in the visible, expressed elements on the inside and outside of the building. Huge steel ducts penetrate the taut white skin of the roof; inside, industrial-scale flues vent fresh air into the Dome from the top of each internal core building. Round the perimeter, twelve dark-blue metal canisters raised up on legs house the primary plant behind open screens, theatrically lit at night to reveal the working elements. The image is of a powerhouse, a gathering place of energy, with evocative undertones of naval or aeronautical design.

From the brightly coloured external ducts and vents of the Pompidou Centre, to the gleaming steel external servicing of the Lloyd's Building, expressing the plant has been a notable feature of the work of Richard Rogers Partnership. Practically speaking, putting the servicing outside the building provides a flexible internal layout, a flexibility that has always been a requirement of the Dome. But there is an aesthetic at work, too, an aesthetic concerned with honesty rather than concealment, together with an equivalent design commitment to acknowledging the vital role of these engineering elements.

As the preliminary ideas for the servicing infrastructure developed, the concept evolved of the Dome as a 'little town centre', a town centre that just happened to have a cover on it. The quadrapod bases of the twelve steel masts had always been designed so that emergency vehicles could pass below – in fact, the bases are so high that articulated lorries can be driven underneath. The resulting circular route or 'main street', which would become the main pedestrian circulation path round the interior – known as Mast Way – not only provided a useful analogy for the servicing design but was one of the earliest fixed points of the Dome's internal layout.

Designing the internal environment

A key part of the early design process was imagining what it would feel like inside the Dome. The design of houses or conventional buildings

generally raises no such issues: we all know what it feels like to be indoors on a winter's day with the heating turned up, or on a summer's day with the windows open. These are known, predictable parameters. In the case of the Dome, however, no precedents existed that could have provided a point of comparison.

For Tony McLaughlin, who leads the environmental and building services team at Buro Happold, that was the joy of the challenge: 'That's what was interesting to me and everybody else in the team. What made it even more interesting was that we were trying to decide what the environment was without a brief.' He adds: 'As engineers we're always looking for precedents, and we also tend to be cautious. That's what the public expect of engineers. But the way we work at Buro Happold is when we come to something that's new we throw the shackles away. We throw away the regulations, we throw away the book, really, and say, "let's start at the beginning". We try to come up with engineering thought that is different, that is going to add to the finished product and

not play a subservient role to it. Then, when we get something we like from an engineering point of view, something that can also relate to the aesthetic of the architecture, we have to come back into line again and start applying the rules, the fundamental laws that all engineering is bound by. At the end of the day if we come out with our concepts intact then we feel good.'

Environmental issues started to surface as soon as the design was developed. It was not merely a question of the Dome's designers worrying about it, the client, the relevant government ministers and almost everyone else involved wanted to know what it would be like inside. Would it be hot? Would it be cold? Would it be draughty? Would people be comfortable? In the early stages only a few pieces of the

Designing the Dome's servicing – determining its internal environment – was a considerable technical challenge which fell to the Buro Happold engineers.

jigsaw were in place. It was known that up to 35,000 visitors were expected a day, that the door element was envisaged as being minimal to encourage a free flow and that the interior would be filled with exhibits, each generating a great deal of energy. At the same time, both for economic and environmental reasons, there was the desire to make the Dome as energy-efficient as possible. The fundamental objective was to put as little energy as possible into heating or cooling the air.

A critical factor in the perception of comfort is air movement. An environment with moving air will always be perceived as cooler than one where the air is still. The designers worked at ways of enhancing natural ventilation with strategically placed fans. The masts had always been designed to incorporate fans but analysis had indicated that these would not provide the degree of extract required on warm days – bearing in mind that the Dome encloses some 2 million cubic metres of air and requires a minimum of one complete air change every two hours.

Resolution of this problem came at the same time the central hub was changed to the 30-metre cable ring. As Ian Liddell recalls, it was a 'bit of instant design'. One evening, when he and Tony McLaughlin were discussing the ventilation and the problem of getting rid of the heat gains within the Dome in the summer, it suddenly occurred to them that this central ring could be filled with opening vents. The resulting assembly, of 36 louvres and 12 fans, immediately provided the dynamic air movement that was required, helping to generate a 'stack effect' whereby rising warm air in the centre of the Dome escapes through the top vents and pulls fresh air in through the openings at ground level.

This design decision came in February 1997. The provision for the opening vents had to be included in the cable contract at that time. The decision was initially based on Tony McLaughlin's back-of-the-envelope calculations; subsequently, more detailed analysis (including computational fluid dynamics) proved that the engineers had been right in their estimations.

The engineers had to decide what the environment would be like, but they also had to determine how much power would be needed, how much cooling and heating, and how servicing could be provided in a flexible, practical way. Working from initial 'hand' calculations and progressing to simple two-dimensional thermal analyses, they were eventually able to produce an incredibly sophisticated three-dimensional computer model, so powerful it had to be run on the Atomic Energy Authority's computer at the Harwell plant in Didcot. Three-quarters of a million cells were required to generate the image, compared to 25,000 for a normal building, with each cell originally more or less input by hand. Using computational fluid dynamics, this huge model was able not only to investigate different environmental conditions given variations in outside air temperature, wind speed and so on, but could also take into

Inside and out, the Dome expresses its servicing elements. Huge industrial flues mounted on the roofs of the core buildings push fresh air into the interior *(above and right)*. Such elements are standard components, with slight design modifications.

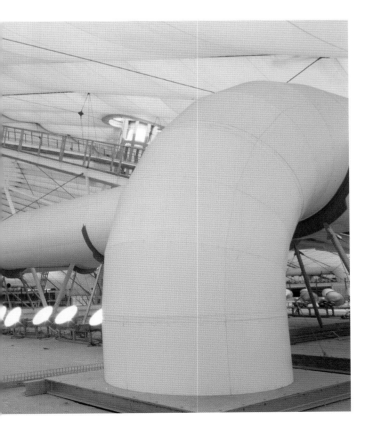

The central cap assembly of 36 opening louvres and 12 fans promotes dynamic air movement to keep the interior of the Dome at a comfortable temperature. It was manufactured by British firm Baco and installed from the top of the central scaffolding.

account the impact of all the interior structures on the microclimate of the Dome as a whole. Air flows and heat transfer flows could both be modelled to come up with a full picture and the results presented in diagrammatic form. Some idea of the level of complexity involved can be gauged from the fact that each time the engineers wanted to analyse a particular situation, it took four days for the computer to come up with the results.

How do you quantify the unquantifiable? Comfort is a notoriously relative and elastic concept. As the designers' ideas developed, it became clear that the most sensible approach was to consider the Dome's environment as neither fully interior nor fully exterior, but something between the two. Visitors to the Dome should not immediately perceive it as a different climatic environment. Ideally, each visitor's first impressions should be of the exhibition itself and not a sudden variation in temperature. A useful analogy is that of a railway station or shopping centre, similarly enclosed areas which moderate the weather but not to the extent that people immediately wish to shed their outdoor clothes. Within the 'umbrella environment' of the Dome, the more enclosed areas of the exhibition structures would be where extra cooling or heating would be targeted. The computer model helped to identify trends and detect problems, such as pockets of dead air where more movement was required, or areas where the heat levels appeared too high.

The bean cans and the infrastructure

At the early stages of the design, as the planning submission was being prepared, designing the servicing infrastructure – the hard elements, the ducts, the cables, the power supply – proved to be just as much a leap into the dark as the foundation design had been. There was still no fixed idea what would be happening in the interior. Heating, lighting, cooling, communication, water and drains would be required, but where? As with the foundations, the only sensible answer, which allowed for future developments, was to come up with some sort of flexible arrangement whereby the exhibitions could be plugged in as the need dictated. The circular form of the Dome suggested a radial system, with servicing entering the structure at the perimeter and connected in a network circumferentially inside. A fully flexible network, however, would have been extremely costly and, equally important, could not have been constructed in the timescale.

The answer was to distribute the servicing from six primary 'core' buildings inside the Dome, which would also be the location for the information infrastructures, main toilets and restaurants. From these six core buildings, six radial trenches about 6 metres deep by 1.5 metres wide, would carry the servicing into the centre of the Dome, connected by a number of circumferential trenches. In total, there are now two

Power and mechanical services are distributed in a network of radial trenches connected circumferentially – the circularity of the Dome informs the basic planning of the infrastructure *(above)*. Huge stainless-steel ducts penetrate the pristine skin of the roof, venting exhaust air from kitchens *(right)*.

The servicing strategy at the Dome was to put the primary plant outside the main structure into twelve cylinders *(right, above)*. Affectionately known as the 'bean cans', these cylinders were originally conceived as the silver spheres of the Circle of Time. In their new hard-working role, they house a variety of bulky, noisy plant out of the way. Going underground – power and chilled water from the chiller units in the cylinders is routed back into the core buildings where the secondary plant is located *(above, below right and far right)*.

kilometres of services trenches, divided into three, carrying mechanical, electrical and data/communication servicing.

Designing the servicing infrastructure involved long strategic discussions. An important issue was where to place the primary plant – the high-voltage switch gear, the chiller units and so on. The objective was to get the roof covering up as quickly as possible. Manufacturing a large servicing plant off the site and then bringing it into the Dome would have impinged on the programme. It would also have taken up room that could be better used as exhibition space.

In the original Imagination concept, twelve silver spheres, the Circle of Time, were arranged round the perimeter of the Dome. The idea had been to use the spheres as touring exhibitions to involve the regions in the project, then bring them back to the Dome for the exhibition year. Although this proposal had been ruled out in the early stages on the grounds of cost, Mike Davies had always been keen to keep the spheres because they formed an essential counterpoint to the scale of the Dome. The problem was that the spheres had no role. 'I loved the spheres as icons and wanted to protect that vision,' says Mike Davies. 'They represented an element of articulation against the huge scale of the Dome, an important transition in terms of scale. After it became clear that they were not viable as exhibits, we realized that unless we made them a requirement, they would disappear.'

Then, when Buro Happold came to the conclusion that they needed somewhere outside the Dome to put the primary plant, an obvious answer suggested itself: the plant could go in the spheres. 'This gelling, when it came together, it came together almost in a day,' says Tony McLaughlin. 'Other things you can sweat over for months and not have the same result. The diagrams were very poetic at that time – one sphere was hot and one was cold. Eventually this was diluted, but your strategy always has to be simple, it has to be read.'

As square pegs do not generally fit into round holes, the spheres then became cylinders – affectionately known as the 'bean cans' – a shape which would better accommodate the type of plant that they had to contain. 'As plant space, the sphere is not a flexible shape,' says Mike Davies. 'Turning the spheres into cylinders meant we could keep the spirit of the idea but it also meant we could stack things vertically in a flexible racking system.' It was a highly practical and cost-effective solution. The bean cans freed up space inside the Dome for what it really should contain and kept noisy plant out of the way, but where it could be easily maintained. Partially enclosed by an outer screen of fins, they revealed the working servicing of the Dome in an honest expression of its engineered elements. 'As a firm, we've always expressed plant as external elements anyway – we've never been afraid of plant on the outside,' says Mike Davies.

Each pair of cylinders contains a variety of primary plant on three upper levels: including chillers to chill the water for air conditioning, high-voltage switch rooms, stand-by generators, fire sprinkler tanks and various pumping systems. These services are then routed in cables and pipes down the middle of each cylinder and then underground to the secondary plant room in the core building. The selection of the plant was informed by consultation with LIFFE (London International Finance, Futures and Options Exchange), who had identified the type of plant that could most easily be sold on in the future.

Each three-storey core building contains two air-handling units to draw in air from outside the Dome, chill or heat it and then duct it into the interior. Another very visible servicing element are the four stainless-steel ducts that penetrate the Dome's roof from behind each core building, and act as the exhaust air ducts for the kitchens and toilets. Four inlet ducts, three metres in diameter, pull fresh air into the secondary plant and push it out through massive industrial flues on the top of each core building. These elements, robust pieces of industrial design, were more or less standard components, just modified slightly where necessary.

> These cylinders have now become part of the image of the Dome. Lit at night they do come across as engineering elements and give a certain aesthetic to it. Of course we have an architect who can take on these sort of things, it's very much their aesthetic. Richard Rogers buy into this sort of thinking.
>
> Dick Coffey, NMEC

Like the fabric of its roof, the choice of HFC (hydrofluorocarbon) gas for the refrigerants in the Dome's chiller units has proved somewhat controversial. Had it proved cost-effective to integrate the Dome's servicing with the servicing infrastructure for the peninsula as a whole, other options might well have been explored. As it was, with the cylinders located in public areas, safety had to be a prime consideration. HFCs have replaced the ozone-depleting gases of CFCs and HCFCs as the standard refrigerants used in 90 per cent of new chiller units. What the environmental lobby prefer, however, is hydrocarbon gas, increasingly used in oil rigs and environments that are designed to cope with potentially explosive gases. At the Dome, the public risk was simply too great to experiment with this new technology. In any event, HFC gas only has an environmental impact if it leaks. Consequently, about £100,000 has been spent at the Dome on continuous monitoring by modem link to check the performance of all the chiller units.

Fire safety engineering

Ninety-nine per cent of all buildings fit within normal building codes, but the Dome broke all prescriptive rules. As with the servicing, making sure it was safe meant taking a step back and looking, not at the rule book, but at the performance actually required by the regulations. The basic principles of fire regulations, for example, are that in the case of fire, people must be able to get out quickly, that there must be proper access for firefighting equipment and that both materials and design should be as fire-retardant as possible. Fire safety engineering meant that it was possible to exceed standards to a far greater extent than if the rules had simply been applied.

Martin Kealey, fire safety engineer at Buro Happold FEDRA (Fire Engineering Design Risk Assessment), remembers the first meeting with Greenwich Council's building control officer: 'He said, "I assume we're not going to use the rule book for this," and we said, "You're right."' In ordinary circumstances, it would be a great deal for a council to take on trust but Buro Happold, who have just written the new British Standard for means of escape, have long been at the forefront of fire safety design.

Like the servicing strategy, the overall approach was to treat the Dome as a small town centre, with its own access roads, fire hydrants and escape routes. The individual exhibits were treated as buildings and rules were devised regarding safe construction materials, escape and access for each zone. The engineers came up with their own rule book, 'The Designer's Guide', which they issued to all exhibition designers, caterers and retailers. Having devised the strategy, their next task was to ensure everyone kept to it. This meant monitoring every aspect of construction and fitting out throughout the Dome's interior.

The strategy itself was based on detailed computer analysis. Using a computer program called 'Exodus' at Greenwich University, the engineers were able to import drawing files from the architects and fill the Dome with 'people' to model escape times. Different attributes could be assigned to the 'people' in the model: variables like age, sex, mobility and emotional response to an emergency. Running the model with different variables each time enabled the designers to come up with a picture of how people would behave. The results of this analysis then fed back into the design of the Dome. By rearranging exit routes, modifying the position of doors in relation to gangways and aisles, and other such changes, optimum escape times were achieved.

Computer analysis was also the means for devising a smoke management strategy. 'Tony McLaughlin modelled the internal environment using CFD [computational fluid dynamics] and once he got that solution stabilized we then set fire to it,' says Martin Kealey. The computer analysis revealed that the Dome's ventilation systems provide a huge capacity for smoke extraction. The 36 open vents work in combination with the 12 exhaust fans to provide a capacity far in excess of that required for safe evacuation of people.

> *We tend to only work on buildings that don't fit the rules.*
> **Martin Kealey, Buro Happold FEDRA**

The 'bean cans' or service cylinders have built-in flexibility. Plant is racked on three levels *(above left)* where it can be easily accessed and maintained *(below left)*. Servicing is routed down the centre of the cylinders and from there to the core buildings *(centre left)*. When lit at night, the cylinders suggest a powerhouse of energy *(right)*.

Expressing the servicing on the outside of the building has always been part of the aesthetic of Richard Rogers Partnership. The metal fins that encircle the cylinders only partially screen the working elements, and could easily be removed in the future if additional or different plant were required. But in addition to their practical role, the cylinders provide an essential counterpoint to the scale of the Dome, a role emphasized by theatrical lighting at night.

The environment

For most people, the idea of the Dome being an environmentally friendly structure is a notion which, at best, tends to prompt a hollow laugh. Its public perception as a 'plastic', ephemeral and opportunistic overreaction to a simple change of date has meant that the scheme's potential long-term environmental benefits have rarely been acknowledged. Throughout its short history, the Dome has been battered by a series of single-interest environmental campaigns, campaigns which have found it hard to resist the tempting transposition of 'doom' and 'dome'. But aside from such exercises in throwing mud and seeing how much would stick, the Dome, perhaps, simply does not fit with most people's image of environmental design: an image derived largely from projects which are smaller in scale, local in context and essentially modest. The Dome is manifestly not modest and it is very far from small. Yet it is precisely these qualities that have provided some unique opportunities both to put across environmental messages and to incorporate high standards of environmental practice.

Surprisingly, given the massive constraints of time and money, and the sheer logistical difficulties faced by the project, the Dome has been created within the framework of an equally ambitious environmental policy. 'It's a constraint we have imposed on ourselves,' says Gregor Harvie. One of the conditions agreed with Greenwich Council when planning permission was granted was the preparation of a detailed environmental plan. But the Dome's designers have essentially gone one better, setting specific targets in an attempt to demonstrate that an undertaking of this scale could be developed with environmental concerns very much to the forefront. The high profile of the project has meant they could do no less.

Since the normal 'payback model' of environmental design, whereby the extra costs associated with environmentally friendly building can be set against lower running costs over a twenty- or thirty-year period, simply does not apply in the case of the Dome, the challenge is all the greater. The Dome, in the first instance, is designed to house an exhibition whose duration is only a year. Over that brief timescale, few of the business calculations for using low-energy materials and plant actually work. The result has been the need to come up with an innovative approach to environmental design, with the focus equally on changing attitudes and on tangible, measurable benefits. Key participants in the process have been leading environmentalists Professor Chris Baines, John Elkington, Professor Sir Peter Hall, Professor James Lovelock, the Hon Sara Morrison of the World Wildlife Foundation and Sir Crispin Tickell, who have all acted as consultants to the project.

The environmental plan

Environmental planning began in the early stages of the project. A hundred-page independent study commissioned before the scheme was submitted to Greenwich Council looked at the likely impact of the Dome on the existing environment of the peninsula. The report concluded that given the dereliction of the site, it would be very difficult to make things worse than they actually were.

Rather than use these findings as a convenient excuse to set sights low, a detailed environmental plan was then prepared, which identified a number of key aims, ranging from ensuring that there was maximum use of renewable, reusable or recyclable materials in the development of the project, to minimizing the consumption of non-renewable energy, to enhancing the ecology of the site. These aims were then translated into a series of objectives and achievable, measurable targets. Steps were taken to ensure that the plan was fully integrated into every aspect of decision-making and implemented by everyone working on the project – from contractors and suppliers to designers – and progress was monitored and reviewed on a regular basis. It was not merely a question of ensuring that the Dome, as a structure, was as environmentally friendly as possible, but also of ensuring that its content, the Experience, was sending out the right environmental messages.

The Dome sits on what was until recently one of the nastiest slices of post-industrial landscape in London, a fact that has somehow been perceived as being detrimental to its environmental credentials. Building on poisoned ground is, after all, few people's preferred option. But one of the most important ways in which the project has met its environmental aims derives from this unpromising context. By acting as a catalyst for the decontamination and regeneration, by English Partnerships, of the wider peninsula, the Dome has helped to bring a derelict area back to life. As far as the Dome is concerned, it would have been far easier, for example, to have built it on a greenfield site, but, as is increasingly recognized, environmental best practice today means regenerating brownfield urban sites wherever possible. On the peninsula, more has been spent on roads, servicing, landscaping and regeneration of the river edge – features that provide a long-term legacy – than on the structure of the Dome itself. 'There is actually more money in the ground than above it,' says Gregor Harvie.

Until 1997 a derelict site, the area to the south of the Dome has been transformed into extensive public parkland – urban greening in practice.

The Dome itself does not appear to be an environmentally friendly building; it doesn't look the part. It isn't made of wood, wattle or thatch; its materials are high-tech and industrial: steel and glass-fibre fabric coated with a space-age finish. Its roof is not punctuated by solar panels, nor does a wind-farm hum nearby. Appearances, however, can be deceptive. Because the Dome's structure is so light and uses the minimum of materials, its environmental cost in terms of the energy used to manufacture and transport those materials is also minimal; it represents a very energy-efficient way of covering such a huge area. Minimal energy is also being put into the Dome to heat or cool it. With a translucent roof providing daylight conditions indoors and servicing designed to target treated air specifically to those areas most in need of climate moderation, the energy consumption of the Experience is also minimized as far as possible. Much of the servicing plant used in the Dome could either be adapted to future uses or sold on after the Experience is over; materials unused during construction and wastes generated during operation are sent for recycling or reuse. The Experience itself has been designed so that many of its components could be reused after the show was over, with individual exhibits given to schools, or exhibition materials such as fabrics recycled as temporary shelters for the homeless, for example. Some exhibits make evocative and expressive use of recycled materials; all incorporate environmental messages, and one in particular, the Living Island zone, takes the environment as its overall theme, re-creating a British seaside resort and incorporating a real beach into its contents.

Gardens

'Garden' is not a term one would immediately associate with the areas around the Dome. With 35,000 visitors expected every day, many of these areas are necessarily hard-surfaced. Growing conditions on the peninsula are far from ideal: the site is windy and exposed. The Dome's opening date in the dead of winter, when many species are dormant, has added an extra degree of difficulty to the design task. 'If you call something a garden, people automatically expect roses,' says Dan Pearson, the 'artistic director' of the Dome's planted areas. 'This is more like green ribbons running through the site. Garden is a word that can be applied to all sorts of things.'

The treatment of planted areas, both on the site and on the peninsula as a whole, has provided the opportunity to challenge attitudes about urban green space. While imported exotic species may create splashy, colourful effects, they also often require specialist cultivation. For the planting around the Dome, the deliberate policy has been to use mainly indigenous plants, which individually may be less spectacular, but which work with what can be extreme local conditions, require little additional maintenance or irrigation, last better and encourage biodiversity by supporting native species of wildlife.

On the design side, too, the aim has been to change traditional attitudes about what public planting should be: 'What we're trying to do is to point out that large-scale "municipal" planting doesn't have to include things you've seen before,' says Dan Pearson. 'We're using lots of ornamental grasses and flowering perennials and trying to push people's ideas forward a little bit.' Existing structural features, lighting, colour and strong graphic elements, such as living poles of willow, help the planting to register even in the dead of winter.

The gardens at the Dome range from horticultural set pieces to natural habitats, off bounds to the public, reserved for wildlife. Around the site industrial features past and present are being transformed by creative planting. One such is the vent structure for the Jubilee Line extension, which emerges in the middle of the main piazza area in front of the Dome. The conventional approach might have been to conceal the entire structure, but Dan Pearson found it 'quite an interesting architectural feature' in its own right. Hanging Gardens, a living sculpture 8 metres high, has been designed to wrap round the structure like a natural hoarding without completely hiding it. 'The wonderful thing about parks is that people naturally tend to gravitate to greenery to relax and unwind,' says Dan Pearson. 'Hanging Gardens provides a green presence in the area where visitors will arrive.' An exuberant focal point at the Dome's entrance, each face of this graphic, linear garden features a different selection of plants, chosen to suit the differing aspects, a variety of colour and texture theatrically emphasized by lighting.

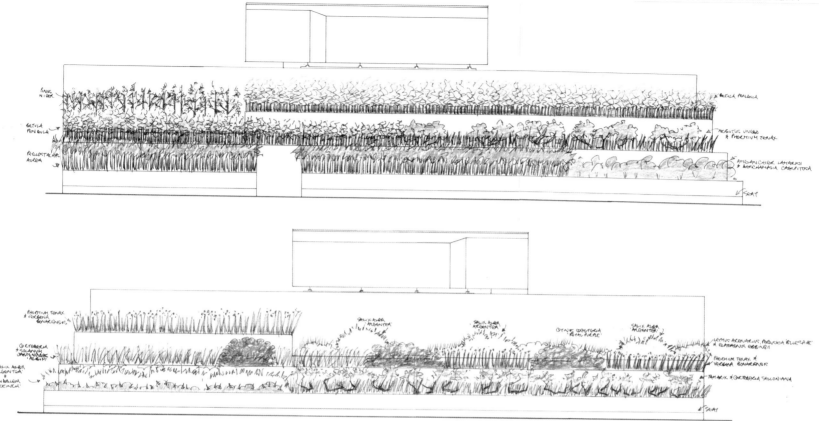

Like the entrance area, Meridian Quarter on the northwest side of the site is necessarily hard-surfaced. A dynamic feature of this outside area is the Living Wall, which serves to link the Dome with the Thames; at its furthest edge, the wall is bisected by the meridian line. A green corridor 5.5 metres high and 180 metres long, the wall is grown up from huge planters, with the horticultural cover clambering over a painted wooden backdrop. Planting, which is more organized and ornamental near the Dome, gradually becomes more naturalistic as it reaches the river edge, a sequence echoed in the shift of lighting style from architectural to more 'stellar' and impressionistic. 'Everything has to be containerized which sets strict parameters, but I hope the planting can be free within those bounds,' says Dan Pearson. Multi-stemmed silver birch is used near the Dome, with natural turf mounds dotted with wild flowers near the river edge.

In practical terms, the Living Wall serves to screen the site offices, which become an operational 'back of house' base during the exhibition year. More evocatively, the wall also incorporates the Watercycle installation, a large waterfall symbolizing the recycling of water at the Dome. The water theme is underscored by the wave form of willow posts inserted into the planting. 'Willow has been traditionally used as a quick fix for stabilizing riverbanks and stabilizing ground,' says Dan Pearson. 'You just stick a piece of willow into the ground and it grows.

A garden for the long term: reclaimed willows sit in bags waiting to be planted on a disused jetty *(below left)*. Dan Pearson's planting plans for the north *(top)* and south *(above)* elevations of Hanging Gardens.

We've found a species of very fast-growing willow which is used for biomass, an alternative source of energy used in two or three power stations in the country. Dormant cuttings taken in 1999 will provide new growth in 2000. It's really a metaphor – taking something from one century and developing it in the next.'

At the river edge, the Living Wall provides a visual connection for a garden 10 metres from the northwestern shore. Airy's Point, one of the first views that river-boat passengers will have of the site, is a disused barge pier formerly known as Ordnance Jetty. Using timber reclaimed from other river structures, a container has been built on top of the old pier and planted with plugs of native species reclaimed from a riverbank site due for development a few kilometres downstream at Thamesmead. Incorporating gravel areas for ground-nesting birds and shallow pools where wildlife can drink and bathe, this island of green re-creates the type of habitat found in tidal estuary flood plains.

'One of the most exhilarating things about this project is that you do a sketch and it's being built almost immediately, says Gregor Harvie.

Local schoolchildren plant 500 reeds at the Dome site to mark '500 days to go!' (*above*). At the Dome, English Partnerships has developed a new riverbank ecology which essentially returns some of the site back to the river and provides a new habitat for native species.

'When we were talking about redeveloping Ordnance Jetty, we had a meeting and we came up with a concept scheme for rebuilding the pier with driftwood and planting it with native species to provide roost sites for migratory fowl. Two weeks later the timber arrived. And these are huge pieces of timber, brought up the river by barge. That's frightening. Somebody had to make that happen.'

The greening of the river edge provides a strong environmental message. Over the centuries, in the quest for land to develop, London has gradually encroached on the river: at the Dome site, the Thames is now under a third of its original width. Part of the remediation of the site was to replace decaying flood defence walls. Working in collaboration with the Environment Agency, English Partnerships has taken the opportunity to develop a new riverbank ecology. New roost and perch sites, as well as niches for invertebrates, plants and algae have been incorporated into the new river flood walls. One specific area of river edge – Blackwall Beach – has been designed as a series of shelving saltmarsh terraces planted with reeds and other marsh-type plants in the intertidal range. The objective is to attract waders and a variety of other native species back to the heart of London. 'We're actually giving a bit of the site back to the river,' says Gregor Harvie. Here the river is nine metres wider than it was; some of the chief beneficiaries are migrating fish, who need places to rest in their journey upstream.

One of the hardest-working garden areas is to the north and west of the Dome. Here, six acres of new landscape, Wetlands, re-creates estuarine pasture, the original habitat of the peninsula before industrialization. Incorporating a wildflower meadow, the landscape has been planted with native species which will mature in five years' time. Boardwalks through the landscape provide viewing points. What visitors will see, however, is not merely for show. Wetlands, the location for reed beds that filter and purify rainwater from the Dome roof, is a functioning landscape. 'Wetlands is fascinating,' says Dan Pearson. 'In our designs for the gardens, we've tried to tie in with Wetlands very carefully, so that everything reads as a whole. Hopefully people will see that there has been a strong intent behind it all.'

The recycling scheme

One of the most innovative environmental aspects of the Dome has to do with the rather prosaic matter of flushing toilets. Under the general aim of minimizing energy consumption, two targets identified by the Environmental Plan were to use low-flush toilets (toilets that use six to seven litres per flush) in the Dome and to flush all 770 toilets on site with reclaimed water. Like everything else associated with the Dome, the scale of the operation brings the whole issue into sharper focus: with 12 million visitors expected throughout the year, one is talking about something in the region of 30 million flushes.

The recycling scheme provides the potential to save a great deal of water, a resource which is increasingly under threat worldwide. 'Most people are now beginning to realize that treating water fit for drinking is an expensive business,' says Peter English. 'Culturally, we only have two sorts of water in this country: clean and dirty. All the water that is clean is fit for drinking and cooking, but only about 5 per cent of it, on the most generous estimate, is actually used for those purposes.' Using reclaimed water to flush toilets is cheaper and more environmentally friendly than using water which has been treated to potable standards, standards that are likely to rise further under European legislation.

> *The exhibition is really about setting standards.*
>
> Peter English, NMEC

The supplier arrangement with Thames Water has enabled NMEC to flush all the toilets in the Dome with reclaimed water from three sources: runoff water from the Dome's roof; recycled grey water from washbasins and showers in the Dome; and ground water obtained from a bore hole. All the sources need treating in different ways.

Collecting runoff water from a roof the size of the Dome provides a spectacular example of recycling in action. Rainwater pours down the Dome's roof, is channelled by special guttering attached to the fabric panels and fed through hoppers to drainage wells at the main anchor points. From here it is pumped to reed beds, located near the new river beach, where natural filtration can take place. 'Reeds have a complex and tight root structure, which acts as a coarse filter,' says Peter English.

Recyling runoff water from the Dome's roof provides a dramatic example of conservation in action *(top)*. Filtered in reed beds located near the river edge, the water is then collected in lagoons *(above)*. All the toilets in the Dome will be flushed with the reclaimed water *(right)*.

Using rainwater as the sole source of reclaimed water, would, however, have required a lagoon the size of the peninsula. The answer was to use not only recycled grey water from sinks and showers, but also ground water. Because London is no longer a city of heavy industry, water is not being taken out of the ground at the rate it was a century or even a half-century ago; the consequence is that underground levels of ground water are rising significantly at a rate of about one metre a year. Tapping ground water helps to relieve some of this pressure. Outside the Dome a bore hole has been drilled 116 metres into the water-bearing chalk beneath the impermeable barrier of London clay. This ground water is then fed into the Thames Water treatment plant on site. When the Dome is sold on at the end of the millennial year, the option is open for the new owner to retain the plant.

Participation is one of the prevailing themes of the Experience. Visitors to the Dome, however, might be forgiven for thinking that interactivity would stop at the washroom door. Yet anyone seeking out one of the 542 toilets in the Dome itself will be taking part in the biggest water experiment ever devised, the results of which could well shape water policy in the next millennium. The great number of visitors and the identical nature of the facilities in the core service buildings provide a perfect basis for comparative research. The Thames Water experiment is designed to investigate the impact of both educational messages about saving water and the effect of state-of-the-art fittings on people's behaviour and water usage. Some of the core buildings have extensive educational messages; some have minimal. Some are fitted with water-saving fittings, such as taps incorporating infrared sensors; others have standard fittings. All washrooms are metered for an accurate comparison to be made of the amount of water people use under different circumstances.

Nor does the story end there. Thames Water are also contracted to remove and treat sewage produced at the Millennium Experience site. Through a joint venture with the Renewable Energy Company they are then generating all the electricity required at the site through sludge-powered generators. This 'Domecycle' is a powerful example of how sustainability can be achieved through partnership.

Transport

Necessity has been the mother of the Dome's transport policy. Realistically, once the Greenwich peninsula was selected as the millennium site, it was immediately obvious that the millions of visitors expected would have to arrive by some form of public transport. Cars were simply out of the question. The main road link from the north side of the River Thames to the peninsula, via the Blackwall Tunnel, is a notorious black spot. Additional road traffic could simply not be imposed on an arterial route that was already over capacity and in an area that was often congested.

Public transport, however, in the case of at least half of the projected visits, would mean the underground, which would mean the Jubilee Line Extension, connecting central London with Docklands and the east. Basing the success of the Dome's transport policy on the delivery of a line infamous for its delay could well be seen as creating a hostage to fortune. While the Dome's deadline might serve as an extra incentive to complete the line on time, NMEC would be able to exert no direct influence on London Underground's programme.

Turning a conspicuous drawback into an advantage has been one of the Dome's best conjuring tricks. Out of a poorly serviced site, with little infrastructure, has emerged an innovative transport policy with an environmental message in its tail: 'Don't drive.' The target has been set for 95 per cent of the visits to the Experience to be car-free, and this is to be achieved by coach, bus, London Underground, river boat, bike or even on foot. Car parking at the Dome is available only for disabled drivers with an orange badge.

Relying on the tube for at least half the projected visits is less high-risk than it might at first appear. Delivery of the Jubilee Line Extension has been planned in three sections: Stratford in east London to North Greenwich (or 'North Greenwich for the Dome in 2000'); Waterloo to North Greenwich; and Green Park to Waterloo, the most problematic part of the line to construct as a result of the poor ground conditions at Westminster. Given the line's huge capacity, with 24 trains per hour, the first two sections alone can deliver enough visitors to the Dome. The journey time from Waterloo takes less than 15 minutes.

The new stations, cathedrals of modern design, represent a striking commitment to the future of public transport. North Greenwich Transport Interchange, designed by Norman Foster, comprises an elegantly curved roof over a bus terminus; below, the largest underground station in Europe, designed by Alsop and Störmer, is faced in a shimmering mosaic of ultramarine tiles.

The Dome's site has provided the opportunity to revitalize a neglected route: the river. New boat operations secured by NMEC to the Dome have provided a kick-start for the government's Thames 2000 Initiative; coincidentally, the whole issue of opening up the river has been a long-running interest of Richard Rogers Partnership. At the north-eastern side of the Dome, a new pier – Millennium Pier – has been constructed on the site of the old coaling jetty at a cost of £2 million. Designed by Richard Rogers Partnership, with marine engineering by Beckett Rankine Partnership and construction by Costains, the pier consists of a floating pontoon anchored to the caissons of the old jetty, and accessed from the riverbank by an 84-metre-long 'canting brow'

Near the Dome, the sinuous curved roof of North Greenwich Transport Interchange, designed by Norman Foster, covers a bus terminus *(above)*, while underground is the largest tube station in Europe. Designed by Alsop and Störmer, elements of its interior are covered in shimmering blue mosaic *(right)*.

which goes up and down on the tide. Towed up the river from Rochester where it was built, the pier brow is the largest in London, and has been designed to allow people with physical disabilities and wheelchair-users to access the pier comfortably, even at low tide.

The river-boat operator, City Cruises, has built four low-emission boats to bring passengers from central London to the Dome. This route starts at the new pier constructed at Waterloo as an integral part of British Airways London Eye millennium wheel and picks up at another new pier at Blackfriars on the north side of the river. The river route has the potential to bring in one million visitors over the year.

On site, as well as 290 parking spaces for coaches and the North Greenwich transport interchange, there is also the terminus of the Millennium Transit link to Charlton railway station on the North Kent Line, served by a new generation of environmentally friendly transport vehicles, part funded by NMEC. These distinctive low-emission buses have low floors and are partly electronically guided. Secure storage for motorbikes and bicycles, with lockers for helmets, is also provided for those who choose to cycle to the Dome along the extended and improved Thames Path, another of the project's 'legacy' items.

Away from the site, it has been a question of discouraging people from driving to nearby areas and hoping to park. As one of the conditions of the planning approval, NMEC has contributed £1.75 million to the setting up of a controlled parking zone in Greenwich to protect local residents and businesses. There are park-and-ride schemes for those who choose to start their journeys by car, but these operate from the periphery of London, rather than close to the Dome.

Transport, as the entry point to the Experience, has a crucial impact on people's enjoyment: the objective has been to provide not only a range of options, but to coordinate the various journeys so they can be managed in a seamless way. One of the most critical aspects of the transport strategy, from the point of view of the ease and convenience of the visitor, has been the development, in association with various transport and tour operators, of travel 'packages' so that visitors, for example, in Manchester, have been able to buy a train or coach ticket to London, connections via tube or river boat to Greenwich, accommodation if required and entry to the Dome in one single transaction. This integrated approach, which offers value for money as well as simplicity, might just serve to reverse some of the negative associations public transport has acquired in recent years. 'This is the first major international event that has taken a public transport approach,' says Sarah Straight, head of transport policy at NMEC. 'It may well be the way things are done in the future. It's an exciting challenge – like everything else about the Dome, it's all about changing attitudes. We want transport to be a positive part of the day out.'

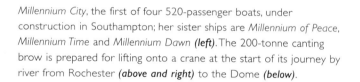

Millennium City, the first of four 520-passenger boats, under construction in Southampton; her sister ships are Millennium of Peace, Millennium Time and Millennium Dawn (left). The 200-tonne canting brow is prepared for lifting onto a crane at the start of its journey by river from Rochester (above and right) to the Dome (below).

Creating the
Experience

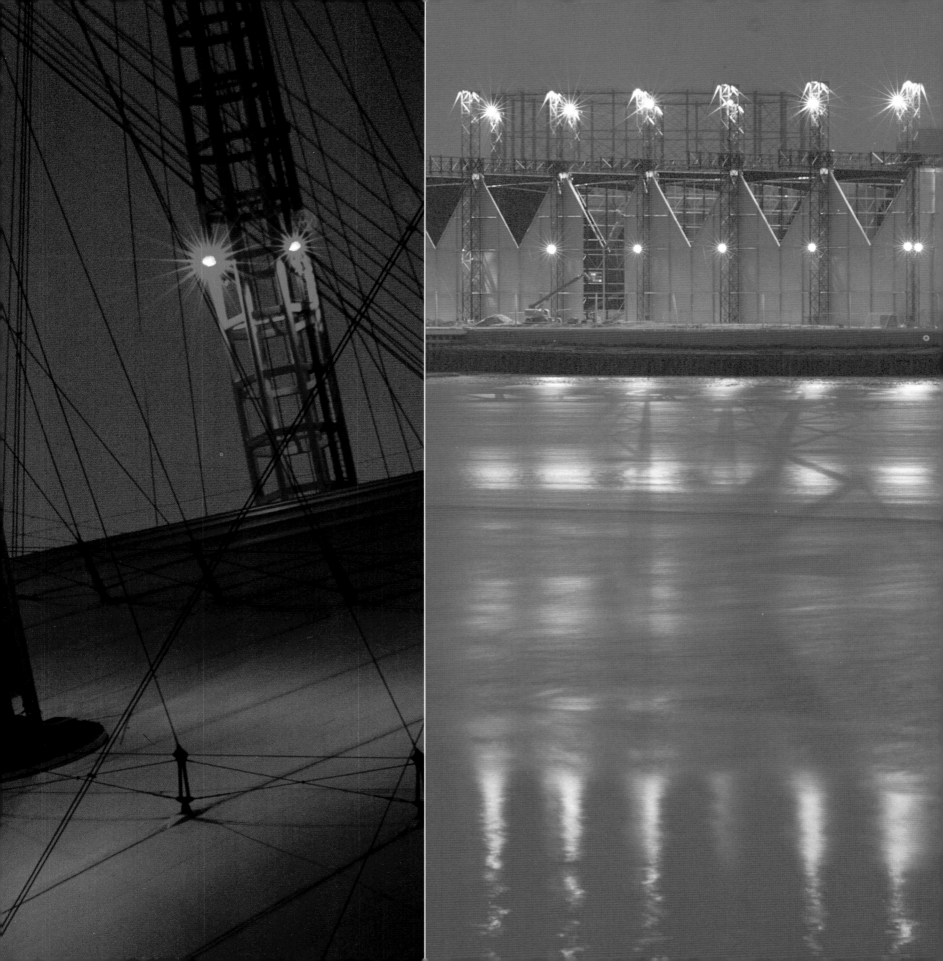

The vast enclosure of the Dome provides a rare spatial experience. The scale is exhilarating; the logic of the geometry generates a strong central pull. As is the case with any dome, from St Paul's to Hagia Sophia, one is irresistibly drawn to the hub, to the focal point of the structural tension. But the Dome has not been designed to stand empty.

If the Dome itself has been proved a national punchline, the source of endless pages of knocking copy, such scorn has been more than matched by the persistent scepticism expressed about its contents, the Millennium Experience. What will be inside the Dome? Will it be worth the price of admission? Will it be a trade fair, a cynical series of marketing ploys, a theme park? With characteristic national pessimism, the public has prepared itself to be not amused, much less amazed.

Neither the clamour for information nor the simmering doubts have been assuaged when proposals for exhibition zones have been presented at press launches. This is hardly surprising, since many of these proposals have represented ideas in development, points of departure rather than arrival. The Body changes shape, changes sex, loses a baby and finds a partner. Spirit, the zone formerly known as The Spirit Level, metamorphoses into Faith. Zones are not only renamed, they move about; and meanwhile the rumour mill works overtime.

'The constraints and indeed the multiple masters involved in a project like this mean you have to have flexibility,' says Jennie Page pragmatically. 'In any event, if you can't make something work then it's better to cut your losses and move on to a new version.'

If this mutability is the inevitable consequence of creative work in progress, there has also been a deliberate holding back. The renaming of the festival or exhibition as the Millennium Experience was no marketing gloss for a project with a troubled history. It signalled a change of direction. The Experience is not a curated collection of exhibits for passive inspection and appreciation. It has been designed to educate, inspire and invite participation. Giving the whole game away before the doors opened, revealing the denouement on page one, would have diluted this crucial sense of immediacy and taken away at least half the fun.

'This is not a museum, it is not an art gallery, nor is it Disneyland,' explains Alex Madina. 'The Dome is unique in the sense that the way the spaces have been developed has been entirely content-led. People aren't trying to give a monolithic view about where we are at the moment, at the millennium. The Experience is a comment and it's asking you to engage and complete that circle.'

On the one hand, a clear distinction can be made between the Dome and what it contains. In the early stages of the project, this separation critically allowed parallel development, with corresponding savings of time and money. On the other hand, however, the two sides of the

Dome scale – under the vast canopy, the multistorey core buildings resemble toy models. Lights mounted in the twelve steel masts illuminate the main circulation route, Mast Way. Articulated lorries could pass beneath the pyramid bases. To provide site visitors with a scale comparison, a Routemaster bus was driven into the Dome early in 1999 – the Dome's volume is equivalent to that of 18,000 double-decker buses.

equation are profoundly enmeshed. Hardly anyone working on the project in a senior capacity has had a job description that is truly watertight. If designing and constructing the Dome had demanded a complex choreography of teamwork and the interweaving of many different disciplines, the final drawing together of structure and content was itself something of an organizational and creative challenge, to say the least.

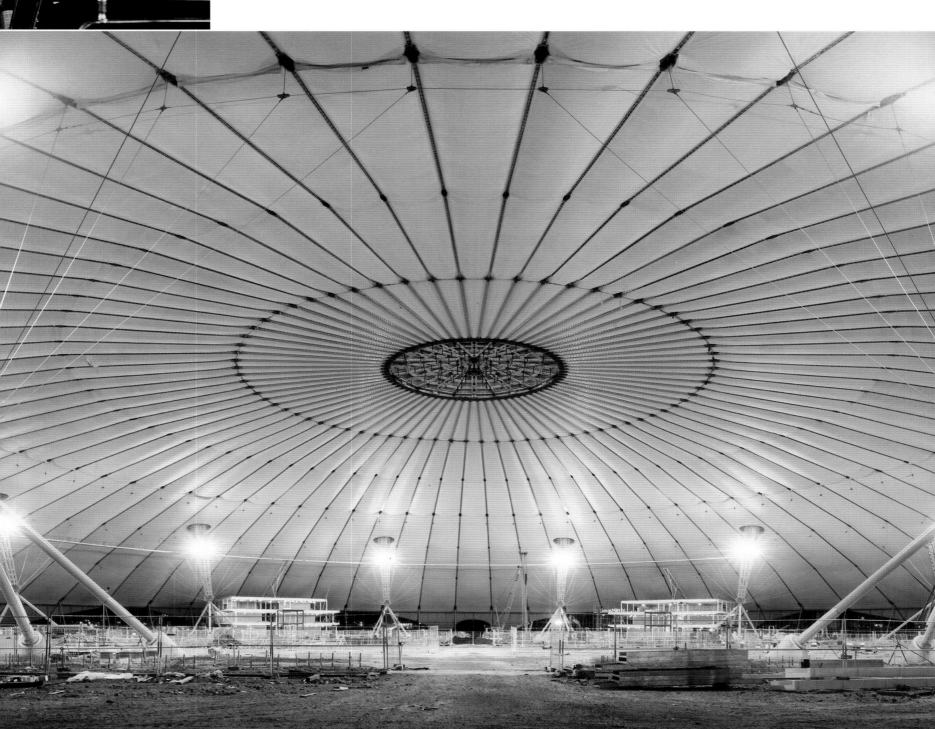

Time to make a difference

Dates that loom large on the calendar instinctively prompt reflection on what has gone before. The very earliest ideas about the national festival had the same backward-looking slant; as the project progressed, time was adopted as a natural theme. It was a theme that needed definition.

In February 1997, when the company was first launched, NMEC commissioned some detailed market research to go back to first principles and determine what people actually thought about the millennium and what they wanted it to signal. Was it viewed merely as a frivolous event, to be marked by parties and fireworks? Was it a time for looking back or looking ahead? Was it a time for serious reflection? The results of the surveys revealed that, in addition to surface cynicism and indifference, there was a strong desire for the millennium to mark a change for the better, a brighter hope for the future. This notion – 'Time to Make a Difference' – provided the central proposition for the new brief. As Claire Sampson, production director of the Experience, remembers, the concept immediately gave a heart to the proposals: 'For the first time we had found a way of articulating the momentous feeling we had about the project.' It was not a static marking of time, but a more dynamic, involving and forward-looking direction.

The exhibition pavilions had originally been themed in a more or less standard way, around topics such as sport, the arts, leisure and so on. What was needed now were subjects that were more inspirational and that could both be expressed within the context of 'making a difference' and provide a more obvious means of linking with sponsorship. After several days of furious brainstorming nine core ideas for zones emerged: Body, Mind, Spirit ('who we are'), Work, Rest, Play ('what we do') and Local, National, Global ('where we live').

The next step was to secure the best design talent. With two later exceptions (for the Talk and Journey zones), it was decided that, given the need to operate within the rules of public financial accountability, the designers would be contracted directly by NMEC rather than by the sponsors. At the beginning of June 1997, expressions of interest from designers were invited Europe-wide and several hundred responses poured in from the usual suspects – 'mad architects', designers of trade stands and thrill rides – along with more appropriate and potentially more interesting groups. A short list was drawn up which included large companies with exhibition or production experience and smaller groups who were less well known but looked as if they might have intriguing ideas. Fifteen-page briefs were prepared on each of the zones, detailing general aspirations on the balance between education, information and fun each zone should provide, as well as parameters such as space, size,

vista and through-put of visitors. The larger companies were given briefs relating to two zones; the smaller companies were given briefs for single zones. The aim was to have four to five proposals for each zone to evaluate. Stimulus questions were also posed regarding the other zones. 'What really surprised us was not a single group came back wanting to tackle a different zone,' says Claire Sampson.

The designers were paid to undertake six weeks of research and design work, come up with models, presentation material and give an indication of budget and staffing proposals. Intellectual property rights agreements were negotiated up front, 'so we couldn't be blackmailed by a good idea'. Once the pitches were in, the final selection of designers was made – and some were paired with different zones where their particular expertise seemed better suited. By October 1997, contracts were in place and the show was up and running.

Or so it seemed. In fact, the project was about to be sidetracked by issues relating to the development of the central area. With the perfect vision of hindsight, it was perhaps an avoidable sidetrack and its unfortunate consequence would be the loss of more time off an already tight programme. But it is in the inevitable nature of design development that avenues have to be explored and what seems at first promising can end leading nowhere.

The central area had always been envisaged as a place to hold a big show which would provide 'one shared experience' within the multiple attractions of the Dome. After the project was given the go-ahead, Sir Cameron Mackintosh, the theatrical impresario with a track record of West End hits, was invited to look at the creation of this central attraction. As the months went by, the ideas for the show acquired something of a centrifugal force, drawing more and more into the middle. A drum theatre was proposed, enclosing the centre of the Dome to provide a blacked-out area for performance; the show grew in scale and escalated in cost until the inevitable happened. The budget for the show was rejected, the scheme was dropped and Sir Cameron Mackintosh resigned. Ten months into the project, a yawning gap had opened up in the middle.

'I was always very torn,' says Claire Sampson. 'The drum theatre would have been a fantastic performance space, but in completely the wrong place. It was an architectural nightmare; it would have been wrong to build a wonderful open space and then put a biscuit tin in the middle of it.' In Jennie Page's view, getting rid of the drum and all the expensive structure associated with it was one of the best things that happened from the point of view of the visiting public.

Designers of the Experience: *(above, from left)* Alex Mowat (Skyscape), Tim Pyne (seated; Living Island, Work and Learning), Nigel Coates (Body), Tim Norman (Skyscape); *(right, from left)* Andrew Partridge (Our Town Stage), Shirley Walker (Play), Alistair Petrie (Talk), Lana Durovic (Talk), Derek Tuke-Hastings (Home Planet) and Mike Davies (Rest and Our Town Stage).

Many of those working on the project could not disguise their relief. The architects, in particular, had struggled to keep their nerve in the face of mounting frustration as one of the unique qualities of the Dome – its breathtaking volume – threatened to be eaten up by a large structure planted in the middle. And this particular cloud, with its associated rainstorm of publicity, also proved to have a silver lining as far as the exhibition design was concerned. The loss of the drum theatre shrank the show down to more manageable proportions and freed up extra space inside the Dome for the zones. 'Everyone's entitled to a learning curve, and mistakes have pretty much been openly declared,' acknowledges Mike Davies. 'In trying to achieve a solution, we've had some false starts, but overall the team has been powerful enough not to go too far down blind alleys.'

Another working relationship was terminated around the time the drum theatre withdrew from the stage. In summer 1997, Stephen Bayley, formerly the director of the Design Museum, had been brought in to advise on the creative development of the exhibition. His watching brief was to keep an eye on the design integrity of the Experience; his persuasive arguments in favour of the selection of the architects Zaha Hadid and Eva Jiricna helped to secure their innovative design talent for the Mind and Faith zones. Bayley's resignation in early 1998 was not entirely, however, a bolt from the blue. Superficially provoked by Peter Mandelson's trip to Disneyland, it had been preceded by private doubts aired in public about the project's direction. By his own admission not a teamworker, and inclined to shoot from the hip, his departure ultimately revealed a clash of personalities as much as creative differences.

From pizza to glue

The drum theatre would have occupied the entire central area of the Dome up to the ring of masts. When the idea was discarded, there was potentially room for more zones, and more zones meant more sponsors and increased visitor capacity. 'Ken Robinson and I had a very entertaining evening where we played about with lots of highlighter pens and some old plans and tried to think about how we might be able to best use the space,' says Claire Sampson. The result was the first 'pizza plan', an internal arrangement of the Dome's interior, allocating notional areas to the zones and defining the amount of space which would be dedicated to the central show. The general idea was that the new, smaller central area should be treated rather like a European piazza, with cafés and informal entertainment providing interest between scheduled shows. A brief was also drawn up about the balance envisaged between seating and performance space and the architects were brought in to structure the concept.

The key aim was to retain the open aspect of the Dome and make full use of all the floor area. In response, the architects came up with the idea of a circular viewing ramp 8 metres off the ground to form a partial enclosure for the centre, with seats coming down towards the middle on one side of this walkway and room for more zones on the other side. A series of bridges was conceived to link the core service buildings to the ramp. There was also a hydraulically lifted drawbridge interrupting the walkway on the axis of the main entrance to provide height clearance and overspill space for special events such as the opening ceremony. The inner ring of the ramp – High Way – complemented the outer main pedestrian circulation route under the masts – Mast Way. The aerial connections of the bridges, like the pyramid bases which straddled the main internal road, added dynamism but also provided a means of getting people higher up into the volume of space. For the first time, the simplicity and power of the Dome's structure was matched by a clarity of internal layout.

Mike Davies explains the dynamic of the central space: 'The promenade is a very basic structure, with the most economical steel detailing possible, but I'm very glad we've held on to the height. Getting 8 metres off the ground makes a huge difference to the feel of the space. At the same time, there's tremendous focus and compression in the Dome. Everyone wants to stand in the middle. The main entrances to the central arena have been kept deliberately low and small – that is, relatively speaking, you can still drive two trucks through alongside each other. But because the entrances aren't really grand, when you come through into the middle, there's a great sense of expansiveness. When it's full of people and beautifully lit it will be very spectacular.'

After the drum theatre idea was discarded, the interior layout of the Dome was reconfigured to provide more room for exhibition zones with an open performance space in the middle. The new layout was sketched out in the first of many 'pizza plans' *(far right)*. A circular walkway, 8 metres off the ground, surrounds the central space and provides a vantage point from where visitors can see across the Dome's expanse.

If the Dome was a pizza in plan, it was also a clock. The six core buildings, one of which is slightly larger than the others to incorporate VIP facilities and a viewing centre, are numbered in their clockface positions: 1, 3, 5, 7 (the larger core), 9 and 11. Between each core were two natural spaces for zones; 9 in total, taking into account the enclosure of the tunnel vent which sits between Core 7 and Core 9. Entry points had been planned along radial routes running between pairs of anchor blocks and entering the structure between the core buildings. The main entrance, at clockface position 6, between Cores 5 and 7, was originally planned to run between the anchor blocks in the same way, but this was felt to be too constricting and it was moved sideways and reconfigured to make a larger and more open access with a better and more accessible relationship to the tube station.

The pizza plan was prepared immediately before the first public 'content' launch on 24 February 1998, when proposals for six of the original nine zones were presented: Body, Mind, Spirit, Rest, Work and Living Island. With the exception of Living Island, nearly all of these zones have subsequently changed, either in appearance or more radically in terms of content. The Work zone, sponsored by Manpower, included a substantial area devoted to lifelong learning and its relevance to the changing world of work. As it was becoming clear that this was simply too much content for one zone and there were also sponsors keen to be associated with education, two days before the launch, Work spawned Learn. The twin zones were paired in the large space beside Core 7 which had resulted from moving the entrance, with their physical links underscoring the conceptual message of learning through life.

Then the ten zones became fourteen. While the outer ring of ten zones had potentially better shaped and larger footprints of up to an acre, there were height restrictions from the sloping roof of the Dome. On the other side of Mast Way, ground area was more restricted, but structures could be higher. Making use of the space freed up by the loss of the drum theatre, the four new zones, located on this side, were Money, Talk, Journey and Self Portrait, a study in national identity. Two of these, Talk, sponsored by BT, and Journey, sponsored by Ford, have been designed by Imagination, working under direct contract with the sponsors, with whom they had close professional relationships.

The basic framework for the Experience was beginning to fall into place, but there was much more reconfiguration, redefinition, renaming and general fluidity to come. From the outside, it all looked faintly comical, like a game of musical chairs where the chairs kept changing shape. From the inside, it (sometimes) made perfect sense. The process required integration and coordination between vastly different

The Dome's roof served as a huge screen for a visual projection launching the Talk zone, sponsored by BT, in a presentation made in October 1998 *(above)*. A certain fluidity has marked the development of the Dome's content – here is the model of the Body zone in one of its earlier forms *(right)*. Note the scale of the human figures compared to to the mammoth 'parent' and 'child'. The baby's nappy provoked considerable debate. Should it be a disposable nappy or an environmentally friendly terrycloth one? Was a nappy necessary at all?

disciplines to achieve the right balance: content that offered designers creative freedom but could be built within budget and on time; content that would educate and inspire, but also entertain and amuse; content that would satisfy sponsors' requirements but not be commercially driven; content that would maintain the integrity of the architecture but provide an enjoyable and safe day out for visitors. It was a process that would have driven anyone mad, had it not been so stimulating.

In Mike Davies' view, the process was emphatically not design-by-committee. 'We all have to be tough to move things forward and make crisp decisions. But we're remarkably compatible as a group. There's a certain bonhomie even when we're having major scraps. Although the process is much more evolutionary than revolutionary, it isn't design-by-committee or consensus. Quite often clarity will come because one person's view has prevailed. We've learned to respect each other's formal skills, but we've also learned to respect each other's gut feel. There are projects you know will work because everyone is genuinely contributing to the richness of it. The characters here are all larger than life. If the project was in the hands of five faceless leaders, you wouldn't get the loyalty, you wouldn't get the humour, the dedication, the obsessive not letting go; you wouldn't get those sorts of passions.'

People working under pressure to tight deadlines and with impossible challenges tend to develop their own shorthand, an insider's code that diffuses the tension and cuts the monumental task down to size. Thus for those working on the Experience, the Amazonian figure of the corporate logo became 'Nora'; the strategic group set up to oversee creative direction became the 'Litmus Group'; zones acquired 'godparents' to nurture their development and 'expert witnesses' to add their sagacious opinions. Zones also had to provide different levels of engagement for 'paddlers', 'swimmers' and 'divers', or, in translation, for those seeking a quick dip into an experience, those content to go with the flow, and those needing a deeper level of information on a particular area of interest. Then there was the Glue Group, a critical group whose task it was to make decisions, both aesthetic and operational, about how the whole thing held together. A CAD walk-through model of the interior of the Dome, the largest model ever developed in the world, was an important tool in this process.

The monikers might have sounded playful, but the organizational structures did have a serious purpose. The Experience had no creative ringmaster imposing a single vision and no one-line message to peddle. Legoland, for example, might include a range of exhibits and rides, but ultimately it all comes down to pieces of plastic brick. Madame Tussaud's boils down to wax. The Science Museum has an identifiable context. The Millennium Experience has been designed and created to be diverse and varied, to be a lot of different things to a lot of different

people. These organizational structures were an important way of making sure that all the bases were covered.

The Glue Group, where many of these issues were hammered out, tackled a wide range of concerns, from strict politics to the very practical: signage, messaging, colour, company image, marketing, design integrity, massing of built forms, interrelation of zones, buildability, cost, and just about anything else one could imagine. Although membership varied, the ultimate core of the group, the 'Superglue', comprised Jennie Page, Ken Robinson, Claire Sampson and Mike Davies. 'It has been a remarkable process in that the diversity of what we have been working on is huge,' says Mike Davies. 'The real strength of the team is its generalist nature. There's a lot of lateral weaving going on, building stories from lots of little bits. It's almost impossible to convey how complex and diverse that process has been.'

The structure also enabled those creating the Experience to draw on a wide range of expertise. The Litmus Group, chaired by Michael Grade, who is also on the board of NMEC, included leading representatives of organizations as varied as Madame Tussaud's and the Royal College of Art. At fortnightly meetings, the group was presented with no written material, no details of budget or programme, but short visual proposals: 'Just what the visitor would see,' in the words of Claire Sampson. The zone designers took care to make these proposals as evocative and stimulating as possible, indeed a seaside organist serenaded one Litmus Group meeting. The crucial editorial role of Litmus was to react without the ties of responsibility. The 'godparents' assigned to each zone, individuals with a particular interest in the subject area, helped develop the content in depth. 'Expert witnesses', leading figures in medicine, science, the arts and the environment, acted as specialist resources which could also be tapped. According to Alex Madina, content editor and manager of both the Glue Group's and Litmus Group's agendas, the result has been that 'each of the zones has been able to draw on the latest thinking in the country'.

The Dome's £449 million Lottery grant is supplemented by £150 million's worth of sponsorship. The whole issue of sponsorship – the notion of the commercial world getting its foot in the door of a national project – has always aroused a widespread degree of public suspicion, a suspicion heightened by the unprecedented amount of sponsorship required. There was simultaneously an anxiety that not enough sponsorship would be found and an anxiety about how that sponsorship, if it were found, would manifest itself in terms of the content of the exhibition.

While it has become more familiar to see corporate logos attached to what were formerly wholly state-run enterprises over the past few decades, such public and private sector marriages still have the capacity to provoke unease. For NMEC, the stakes were high. Excessive branding on the part of any sponsor would ruin the spirit of the exhibition; at the same time, without recognition, major corporations would be unlikely to come on board. As sponsors were found and paired with zones, broad issues of branding had to be thrashed out at contractual level, right down to the small print, to keep commercial messages to a minimum.

An obvious risk of sponsorship was that commercial imperatives might skew the content developed by the zones. The designers of the Play zone found themselves precisely in this position when a potential sponsor sought to over-influence creative direction. 'We were at kind of an impasse. It was a very uncomfortable position to be in,' says Peter Higgins of Land Design Studio. 'But everyone at NMEC supported us and we were able to go ahead on our own terms.' Often, however, the pairing of zones with sponsors has proved creatively and technically productive. Major firms, such as GEC and BT, with their immense technological expertise, have had important contributions to make to the way different zones could be realized.

The diversity of design talent working on the zones has been part of a deliberate policy to avoid creating a 'one-line show'. For Mark Fisher, the creator of the central attraction, the Millennium Show, this variety has unequivocally been a good thing: 'What's interesting about the Dome's interior is that it has the quality of being like a small town or city with different competing structures inside. I think it is very much stronger for the fact that people like Zaha [Hadid] are competing for attention without someone trying to tell them what to do.'

Although cutting-edge architects, such as Zaha Hadid, Eva Jiricna and Branson Coates, may be familiar to the design-literate, many of the design groups are far from household names. This is not to say that their previous work has necessarily shared a similarly low profile. Spectrum, the company in charge of creating both the Money and Self Portrait zones, produced the Hong Kong handover ceremony. WORK, the design company responsible for Living Island, came up with London's '100%' Design show, now a fixture on the exhibition calendar. One of the four new Earth galleries at the National History Museum is the work of Land Design Studio, whose task in the Dome is to get people playing. What these companies have in common is the determination to integrate architectural structure with the interior function of the exhibition, and to combine education with entertainment. Peter Higgins explains: 'It's a cross between theatre, film, television, exhibition and architecture: it's a real hybrid. It's essentially designing with a narrative.'

> *NMEC is a self-determined, very organic and slightly unusual body of people doing a very unusual job. It's been chaotic at times, but I don't know how it could not have been.*
>
> **Peter Higgins, Land Design Studio**

The narrative of the development of the Play zone has been an all-too familiar story of redefinition under constant pressure. In theory, each design team, working with a content editor, were to progress from fully developed briefs to models and finally to the point where the footprint of the zone could be fixed and foundations built. In practice, the process was often less clear cut. In the case of Play, six different schemes were proposed until the central notion of a 'digital playground' finally emerged. A final crunch point came in November 1998 when the designers discovered that their plot had been allocated to retail space and they would have to shift the whole zone five metres up onto another level. 'We had to start again from scratch,' says Peter Higgins. 'But what's been positive is that we have been forced to refine key ideas.'

If it was hard work getting there, Play will be fun. The nub of the idea is creative discovery, with the twenty-odd games that comprise the zone being devised by leading media artists from around the world, such as Toshio Iwai and the MIT Media Lab. 'Artists have appropriated this new technology and produced work that is much more imaginative than designers of commercial games and CD-Roms generally develop,' says Peter Higgins. 'Play should not be exclusively for children, it's a state of mind.' One installation is an 'intelligent room' where furniture supplies magic words that take children on a journey; another is a fifty-a-side screen game based on ping-pong but featuring cats and a dog. 'We've made the games very watchable. It's been an important design criterion not to differentiate between playing and watching – both can be fun.'

The fourteen narratives or stories – and their titles – were publicly presented in their final form on 14 June 1999: 200 days before the millennium deadline. Many were already familiar from previous presentations – notably Zaha Hadid's gravity-defying cantilevered structure for the Mind zone, with its morphing machine and robot zoo, and the Body zone (by HP:ICM in collaboration with Branson Coates), a 60-metre-long sculpture of an embracing couple whose interior offers a unique view of bodily functions. Others, such as Learning Life, with its sensuround evocation of schooldays, had principally changed their names. But there were also surprises: the giant flying saucer of Home Planet, Park Avenue Productions' interpretation of the Global theme, and the provocative Self Portrait, whose basic premise 'andness' portrays Britain, using symbols selected by hundreds of thousands of people from all over the country, as a patchwork quilt where multicultural influences are added rather than integrated into the national fabric.

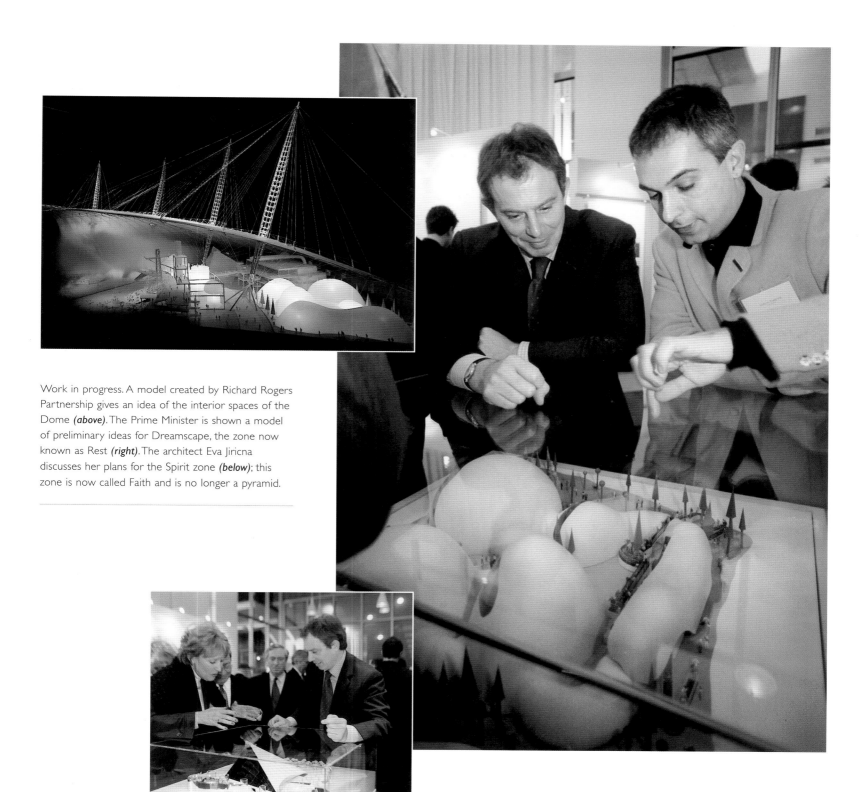

Work in progress. A model created by Richard Rogers Partnership gives an idea of the interior spaces of the Dome *(above)*. The Prime Minister is shown a model of preliminary ideas for Dreamscape, the zone now known as Rest *(right)*. The architect Eva Jiricna discusses her plans for the Spirit zone *(below)*; this zone is now called Faith and is no longer a pyramid.

Inside the Dome

The complexity of the conceptual development of the Experience has been equalled by the intricacies of constructing it. Many of the exhibition structures are buildings in their own right, several storeys high, with lifts, travelators and servicing, not to mention state-of-the-art technological features. As the interior of the Dome filled up with huge steel girders and delivery trucks rumbled round the Mast Way, it was evident that this was no ordinary show in the making.

The point at which the structure of the Dome was complete and control of the site was handed over to those responsible for producing the exhibition could never be a clear cut-off point. As Jennie Page explains: 'We developed a contracting strategy which allowed us to roll out various site and structures contracts to cover the shell and core of some exhibits. So the interface between content and production and site and structures, and between operations and site and structures, is very complicated matter in terms of planning and in terms of managing the shift of control on the site.' For Dick Coffey, it was a question of 'drawing sensible isolation points', gradually reducing the scope for flexibility by grabbing a little more to construct each time. Then there was the logistical nightmare of putting in the support mechanisms for the construction of the zones: arranging the desks and radios, Portakabins and delivery access, as well as coordinating all the individual programmes to meet the final deadline.

> *The difference in a floor finish costing £12.11 and £13.75 doesn't sound like much until you multiply it by 42,000 square metres.*
> **Grant McGregor, NMEC**

Meanwhile there were decisions to be taken about elements of the Dome's infrastructure: choice of balustrading, colour of floor finish, position of lighting and all the other aesthetic and practical features that would create a working environment for the exhibition. One key issue was colour. The architects pressed for a solution that used a family of warm shades – yellow, orange and red – to define different infrastructure elements and give clarity to the interior. Yellow signified the structural elements – the masts. Orange was used to define the areas of movement and circulation – the lifts and stairs. Red was the colour chosen to pick out the six massive lighting towers that ring the central arena. A random combination of all three colours was used for the seats surrounding the arena; the patchwork effect has the advantage of looking lively when the seats are unoccupied but also makes a virtue of the fact that if any seats have to be replaced there is

A family of warm colours – red, orange and yellow – provides a sense of clarity and definition in the Dome's interior. Yellow is the colour used to signify the structural elements of the masts; orange marks out the areas of circulation – lifts and stairs. Red was chosen to pick out the lighting towers that ring the central performance arena.

no need to worry about strict colour matching. For Mike Davies, the strategy 'simplified a lot of complexities'.

Another simplifying factor was the way in which the structure served as part of the Dome's interior furniture. Downlighters in the base of the twelve steel masts lit the main circulation route; directional uplighting mounted on the perimeter masts illuminated the vast canopy. Fans installed under the raked seating of the central arena supplemented the Dome's ventilation systems. This hard-working utilitarian aesthetic, with structural elements playing dual roles, was not only economic, but added to the sense of design cohesion.

As the crescendo of activity built up to fever pitch, one last chore was looming: cleaning the inside of the Dome. When plans were changed for the Dome's interior, and larger exhibition buildings were envisaged, additional piling (1,500 more piles to be exact) was required to act as foundations for these large structures. This piling was carried out in June 1998 after the roof had gone up. The interior surface of the Dome roof is fitted with a fabric liner to prevent a build-up of condensation and the possibility of it quite literally raining inside. The liner material, more porous than the fabric cladding the roof, is also designed to absorb sound. Unfortunately, what it also had conspicuously absorbed was dirt and dust, the inevitable consequence of a covered construction site. Cleaning the liner without drenching all that was below – the fully serviced structures – was a final challenge that faced the site and structures team, led by Cliff Smith of the Joint Venture.

The Dome was filling up, with the bristling metal armature of the Body, with ramps and walkways, bridges, lifts and escalators, with multi-storey structures framed in steel. As the zones came together, the Dome itself shrank. Vistas and views remained, but from one side of the enclosure it was no longer possible to see right across. The Dome had another visual trick up its sleeve. Site visitors who came to inspect progress found it harder than ever to grasp the scale. From most vantage points, the far side of the promenade or elevated walkway appeared to mark the extent of the Dome's diameter, even though another 100 metres extended beyond to the edge of the structure.

BBC children's presenters Richard Bacon and Katie Hill from the television programme *Blue Peter* bury a time capsule at the Dome *(left)*, filled with a variety of objects suggested by young viewers, including a football and, inevitably, the Teletubbies *(above)*.

The structure of the Dome was complete by early 1999, allowing construction work on the structures of the exhibition zones themselves to get under way. Many of these exhibits are buildings in their own right. The metal framework of the Body zone, in the final form of an embracing couple, awaits its lightweight cladding *(above left and above)*; meanwhile the elegant steel arches of the Faith zone are fixed in position *(left)*.

Operations

It is possible to have quite a heated discussion about a litter bin. For Operations, the team who will run the Dome from day one until it closes a year later, getting it right for the visitor meant keeping the details in mind as much as the big picture. Not that details, in the context of the Dome, are ever insignificant. As Ken Robinson, director of operations, explains: 'Multiply anything by 12 million and the answer is always a lot of money.' In the run-up to the opening night, many similar practical decisions had to be taken regarding function, safety, security, cost-effectiveness and, certainly not least, the potential enjoyment of 35,000 people a day. Such pragmatic decisions can cross-cut design intentions. But Ken Robinson says bluntly: 'My role is to raise the pragmatic issues. If it doesn't work, you can't enjoy your day. End of story.'

> *The very best visitor management is management that the visitor doesn't detect. Get it right, so it seems natural and it's probably the very best it can be.*
>
> Ken Robinson, NMEC

From the point of view of operations, details — the placement of seats, critical sight lines, the sense of welcome at arrival — have to be thought through from the perspective of the individual on the ground. If such matters are well considered, they operate on an almost subconscious level — they don't annoy so no one notices them — but if they are wrong, they can undermine the quality of the experience as a whole. The same attitude to detail naturally prevails among designers: the trouble is that the issues and priorities do not always coincide. Set against the designers' inclination to imagine and innovate has been the operational bottom line to predict, anticipate and control. Hence heated discussions about litter bins.

In terms of visitor attractions, what most people hate is uncertainty, delays and queues; they hate being herded at a set pace and they dislike complexity. Equally important, they need facilities — from cafés to lavatories — that are easily accessible. As far as the Dome was concerned, coming up with a strategy that avoided all these negative qualities was perhaps more straightforward than defining how people might enjoy themselves. As Ken Robinson says: 'You can't get library books on this.'

The Experience is unique in that it has not been designed for a particular cross-section of the public, it is intended to appeal to a wide range of people, of different ages and backgrounds, some of whom will want a fairly light-hearted day out and others who will want more involvement and intellectual stimulation. While catering for different needs was an important part of the brief for the zones' designers, it also had operational implications. How do you design a space to provide different levels of involvement but at the same time prevent queuing, overcrowding or bottlenecks? The zones are not analagous to gallery spaces, where people file past exhibits at the pace of the slowest. In the Dome, the shape of individual spaces would have an impact on the way people could interact with what they saw. The role of Operations, in this context, was to look at circulation routes and ensure that there were opportunities for people to pass, stop or move off in a different direction altogether to follow their own interests and take from each zone what they wanted. The Body zone, for example, incorporates a relatively quick experience: an 'intestinal' path that flows through the space. At the same time, there are also 'explore' areas where people can linger and take in information at their own rate. 'It's visitor understanding and visitor needs on top of art and aesthetics,' says Alex Madina. 'It's been a hugely healthy debate. At every design meeting people have almost wanted to have a cardboard cutout of Ken sitting there — they've come away asking themselves what he would think.'

These individual routes within the zones have to be integrated, in turn, within the general pattern of movement in the Dome itself. Here the circularity of the space proved a great asset. Along the main pedestrian route, Mast Way, entrances to the central area allow people to move into the middle and take a break before rejoining the mainstream and visiting new areas. 'The Dome is superb from the point of view of visitor convenience, understanding and clarity,' says Ken Robinson. 'It has been lovely to have that to work with.'

With 12 million potential visitors, the bottom line is to avoid overcrowding in the Dome. Early on, it was decided that all tickets for the Experience would be sold on a prebooked basis, to spread the demand throughout the year and avoid having to cope with a sudden rush in the peak summer months. It was Ken Robinson's inspiration to use the 25,000 Lottery terminals nationwide as the means for booking tickets to the Dome.

Managing 35,000 people a day poses its own operational difficulties. When the concept of the drum theatre, with its huge seating capacity, was rejected, some means became necessary to draw extra people out of the Dome. Although most could be accommodated in the four new zones that the new layout made possible together with the new central

Outside the Dome, Skyscape, comprising two auditoria seating 5,000 people, consists of an externally framed tent. The structure is rented from ESS (Edwin Shirley Staging) and will remain on site for the millennium year only. Skyscape is the venue for a specially commissioned film created by the team behind the popular television series *Blackadder*.

show, about 5,000 people too many would still be inside at any one time. The answer was to create an attraction outside the Dome for which timed tickets could be issued. Thus 'Baby Dome' was born.

In the well-established tradition of Dome naming, Baby Dome is neither a dome nor anything like a baby. For a start, it is a huge entertainment venue comprising two auditoria seating up to 5,000 people, or three times the capacity of Sydney Opera House. Secondly, it has never been a dome. An early visualization of the scheme featured a semicircular shape in the main plaza area; for those working on the project, Baby Dome, what Peter Mandelson called the Dome's apparent 'pregnancy', was a name that simply stuck.

'Skyscape', as it is now properly known, is an externally framed tent some 120 metres long by 60 metres wide and 30 metres high. Developed by architects Urban Salon working in association with Edwin Shirley Staging, who built the Live Aid stage at Wembley, Skyscape is a fabric-clad structure that utilizes part of a pre-existing system; the framework is rented and will be back on the market at the end of the millennial year. Meanwhile it will provide the venue for Dome visitors to watch a half-hour film specially created by the award-winning team

responsible for the television series *Blackadder*, featuring Rowan Atkinson and Tony Robinson in a reprise of their original roles. At night, one of the huge 20-metre-high screens will be removed enabling the space to be used as a performance arena for live music.

Skyscape, immediately adjacent to the new Millennium Pier arrival point is a dominant feature of the plaza area south of the Dome. The treatment of the whole plaza area has been subject to considerable redefinition. With visitors arriving by tube, bus, coach, taxi, bike and river bus, the whole south side of the Dome is geared to processing people: welcoming them to site, orientating them, drawing them into the Dome and serving them with whatever they require in the form of maps, guides, language wands or wheelchairs. 'Just doing that for 12 million people is very difficult indeed,' says Mike Davies. 'We've gone through six plaza concepts with the client before we've reached one that fits the current brief and which fulfils our aesthetic objectives as well.' The solution, which preserves an element of openness while providing protection from the weather, has been to create covered walkways, shielded from sun or rain by 9-metre-square fabric canopies, like a series of fan arches or a Gothic cloister.

Managing a projected total of 35,000 visitors a day poses a considerable operational challenge; clear routes and signage are key factors in visitor convenience. Skyscape, seen to the right of the picture *(above)*, is the venue for timed showings of a specially commissioned film, its two auditoria relieving congestion in the Dome itself.

Countdown

Mid-year 1999, the project was approaching its final deadline. The 300-day milestone came and went; the 200-day milestone passed. There was still a great deal to do. In the spring, over £80 million remained to be spent on the project, a sum, Bernard Ainsworth points out, equivalent to the combined budgets for two or three major construction jobs. On the production side, however frantic the activity, the underlying mood was calm. 'We had to do the best job in the time available,' says Claire Sampson simply. 'I come from a theatre background and in the theatre you're used to working with a fixed end-date.'

The Millennium Show

'I love the whole madness of doing real projects,' says Mark Fisher. Brought in to conceive the event at the heart of the Experience after the loss of the drum theatre, Mark Fisher is the technical wizard behind many rock extravaganzas, and designer of stage sets for Pink Floyd, the Rolling Stones and U2. But his background in architecture has proved as valuable as his track record of creating original visual effects. 'Mark understands the potential of the Dome,' says Mike Davies. 'He can respond to the scale of it. The scale of what he is proposing is Dome-scale not floor-scale.'

'I thought the idea of building the largest covered space in the world and then filling up the middle of it was such a contradiction,' says Mark Fisher. 'I was very pleased to be part of the proposition to do it differently.' The basic strategy for the show was now to keep the centre open, both to preserve views across the space and to allow the centre to be used in the intervals between scheduled shows. But what this also meant was that the show would have to be performed in daylight, largely without recourse to theatrical lighting effects. 'Normally in the theatre, you use the bounds of light and dark to draw the audience's attention. The difficulty with daylit space is that everything, from performers to audience, is equally lit. The bottom line is that the sun is an extraordinarily bright object.' Dealing with the daylight issue was going to mean 'piling in lots of colour'.

The central area of the Dome is about the size of Trafalgar Square. But it is its height at the centre – 50 metres – which is so breathtaking. Part of the thinking behind the show was to draw people's attention up

> *The project is immensely uniting, particularly bearing in mind the amount of opprobrium which has always been associated with it. Those people who are committed to it have felt during the hard times that there is a real purpose and almost a kind of self-justification in demonstrating that the impossible can be done.*
>
> **Jennie Page, NMEC**

to that dizzying height, to 'use the volume of space as part of the performance'. There was one slight difficulty: no one had made any provision to hang anything from the Dome, and a steel maintenance catwalk running round the perimeter had limited the weight allowance in the roof. Mark Fisher's solution was to propose a lightweight aluminium 'bicycle wheel', a circular cage two metres high that could be lifted to the top of the Dome and serve as a platform from which aerial performers could launch themselves into space. 'It is a wonderful piece of engineering made with remarkable economy and speed in Texas,' says Mark Fisher. The bicycle wheel, engineered by Atelier 1, fits snugly under the roof and can accommodate up to 40 people, performers in full costume, along with their technicians and a vast amount of electrical and electronic equipment. 'It will be an asset for the future, enabling a lot of things to be done in the centre of the space.'

Another early decision concerned access for the ground-based performers. By enlarging one of the service trenches, a 'tunnel of lions' was created running from an area near the back-of-house to a corridor under the promenade, so that performers could emerge in the central space without wending their way through the audience and giving the game away. 'A reasonably athletic ferret could make it down there,' says Mark Fisher, although the performers' access has proved to be less a tunnel of lions and rather more of an obstacle course after necessary fire doors were put in.

In the centre of the performance space is a low podium stage, 1.2 metres high, which does not interrupt the views across the arena and serves as somewhere for people to sit between shows. A 5-metre pit, dug under the stage, houses some of the machinery required to put on the show. 'The show needs a crew of 75 to operate it. We've got a whole team of systems engineers just working on the controls,' says Claire Sampson.

What will happen on and above this space between three and five times a day will be an exciting marriage of different entertainment media: part rock concert, part contemporary circus and part modern dance. At Mark Fisher's suggestion, rock legend Peter Gabriel has been commissioned to write the music and is jointly responsible for the conception of the show. Other members of the creative team include

Micha Bergese (personal choreographer to Tina Turner and Mick Jagger) as artistic director, Keith Khan, famous for his flamboyant Notting Hill Carnival costumes, and lighting designer Patrick Woodroffe.

A 180-strong company has been brought together to perform the show, with eighty performing at any one time. Over half these performers are professional dancers, circus artists and aerialists chosen in numerous auditions. The rest, about eighty in total, were recruits to a special training programme devised in association with Circus Space, drawn from varying backgrounds – dance, trampolining, even mountaineering – but an important (and obvious) requirement has been a head for heights and bushels of stamina.

The show will begin with the unfurling of fabric sails to cover the roof of the Dome over the central arena, visually enclosing the space and 'generally taking ownership of it'. From the bicycle wheel, high up in the air, aerial performers will swing, leap and fly into space on quick-release harnesses, dropping down to the ground, clad in articulated, metamorphosing costumes of metal and fabric, where they will be joined by other performers, soloists, stilt-walkers and dancers, while a series of symbolic pieces of scenery will also be deployed to help tell a

A pit 5 metres deep in the centre of the arena houses some of the complex machinery required to put on the Millennium Show *(left and above)*. Much of the show will take place in the air, with performers launching themselves into space from a lightweight 'bicycle wheel' made of aluminium. The wheel is two metres high, 60 metres in diameter, 45 metres up in the air and can accommodate up to 40 people, both aerialists and technicians *(overleaf)*.

fable, 'an allegory with a millennial theme'. Some of these pieces of scenery are so big they extend all the way from the stage right up to the outer edge of the bicycle wheel. With aerialists acting as the theatrical equivalent of abseilers, and kites and sails echoing the aesthetic of the Dome, this spectacular event will literally bring the structure to life.

'These days people get most of their entertainment through the television so the sheer shock of seeing anything modern and live may mean we'll need to hand out cold compresses afterwards,' says Mark Fisher. 'We want to make it accessible. But even so it will probably be quite confrontational for people to see rather sexy and energetic young people doing dangerous and beautiful things only yards away from where they are standing while they are being buffeted by loud rock music. I think NMEC have been remarkably bold to go forward with it.'

Magic

Six months before the biggest deadline in the world might seem an obvious point to call a halt to further development and concentrate on the work in hand. Not so for the Dome. 'There are hundreds of opportunities lurking which we haven't yet exploited,' says Mike Davies. 'This is just the moment to ask what can we do that will surprise us all. My biggest agenda item is more magic between now and December.'

With the zones named, placed, defined and under construction, it was time to turn attention back to the ways in which the structure itself could contribute to the Experience. Ever since he built his own telescope from a lens and some cardboard tubes, and managed to catch sight of Saturn from his parent's garage in north London, Mike Davies has been as passionate about astronomy as he is about architecture. 'The natural world doesn't stop at the edge of the planet. The scale of the universe, the size of the planets and the distances between them are so vast it is difficult for most people to make sensible comparisons. But actually the Dome is big enough to do it. If the Dome were the Sun, for example, the Earth would be a ball 3.5 metres in diameter.' The Dome as a velvety night sky, with stars coming out and comets flashing across from horizon to horizon . . . the Dome as the place where one might encounter Isaac Newton or William Shakespeare face to face and ask them questions . . . these and scores of other ideas provided food for thought in the final months. In true Dome fashion, such embryonic magical concepts have a name: they're called 'smiles'.

Getting a feel for its scale, Millennium Show performers try out their routines for the first time inside the Dome *(left)*. The Dome dons its own red nose for Red Nose Day, marking the BBC charity event Comic Relief *(right)*.

Legacy

We're one in forty.

One in forty generations witnesses a change of millennium, that entirely arbitrary date when history becomes future. Purists may argue, and purists are always right, that the third millennium properly begins at one second past midnight on 1 January 2001, but the date when all four numerals change at once has always been too compelling to ignore. Whichever end of the millennial year people choose to mark this rite of passage, it's a fraction of time. It's the deep breath before the birthday candles are blown out; it's the hush before the peel of bells; it's a wish and a silent resolution worldwide.

The date is arbitrary, shared for practical purposes around the globe, but only one of many cultural new years. In the same way, the Dome has also been arbitrary. It has been a self-imposed challenge, a way of turning what is after all only a momentary turning point into a deadline. It did not have to be built at all. It would have been expedient, convenient and cheaper not to have marked the millennium in such a way. But, ultimately, it would have been a shirking of a responsibility we have not asked for but which we nevertheless share.

That responsibility is to be optimistic, to look forward, to make the imaginative leap ahead and overcome the anxieties and tensions of not only the end of a century, but of the end of a millennium. It's a collective way of whistling in the dark, perhaps, but also a promise we make to the generations who will succeed us.

Optimism breeds optimism, that most unfashionable contemporary state of mind, just as the Dome breeds statistics. Our century has seen momentous changes brought about by technology, changes that have often been bewildering both in their scope and their rapidity. The result has been a widespread suspicion of modernity, a turning away from the present in favour of the nostalgic haven of the past. The millennium presents the opportunity to turn and face the future, to make a difference to the world and the way we live.

The modernity of the Dome lies not in its form but in its 'lightness of being' and in its flexibility. It barely rests on the ground. The result is that its phenomenal size, which is so hard to grasp, is inspiring rather than intimidating: the Dome does not make people feel small. Nor is it a monument whose purpose is fixed in time. 'Modern architecture no longer needs to be monumental,' says Richard Rogers. 'It no longer requires the use of monumental, heavy materials. The Dome is a highly flexible envelope, it's an enclosure rather than a building. With the speed of technology, it's increasingly typical to build before you have a defined brief, for structures to be put up very fast and to change their use very quickly. I often tell my students that there's a nightclub in Rome which is in a church. So what's the best form for a nightclub? What's the best form for a church?' On this level, the legacy of the Dome rests in its innate ability to change its spots, to accommodate what changes lie ahead.

It is a legacy that has been deliberately accounted for in the design process. Problems have been tackled as far as possible from the long-term point of view, not from short-term priorities. The cylinders which house the plant, for example, are half full and could accommodate not only different types of plant, but more plant should the future need arise. Roof panels could be replaced or removed – the middle of the Dome could be taken out, with the edges left as shelter. Trees could sprout through the canopy and solar panels could be installed. Properly maintained, the structure has the potential to last as long as anyone wants it to, and as long as it has a use.

Before a single ticket had even been printed, the process by which the Dome would be sold was already under way. If it was difficult to put a price on the construction of the Dome, setting a sale price was no easier. What is a Dome worth? More to the point, how should it be used? Mike Davies, for one, is buzzing with ideas. 'It's the wrong way round to find a use for the Dome,' he says. 'We have to find a use that grows out of its context and its position on the peninsula, a use that only the Dome can facilitate.'

That position is itself a critical part of the Dome legacy. For too many years, London has sorely neglected its river. The 'beads on a string' concept of bringing the river back to life by intensifying key points along it has recently emerged as a philosophy of the city's planners

and developers. 'One of the biggest beads is Greenwich and the Dome,' says Richard Rogers. 'It's very much about making connections with London life and the life of the nation.' Equally, that position is symbolic, almost virtual. The Dome happens to be in London, but it is by no means London's Dome. Networked to every part of the country, by a programme of activities as well as the computer linkage of the web, the Dome represents a way of reaching out to the widest community possible. Circular in spirit, rather than linear, the Dome is ultimately neither hierarchical nor site-specific.

As far as figures are concerned, you can quantify the legacy of the Dome on any kind of contemporary calculator imaginable. It represents thousands of new jobs brought to the immediate Thames area, and millions of pounds of tourist income; it has brought hundreds of acres of polluted, derelict land into regenerated use; it can be sold on and it will remain part of the London landscape for many years to come. Eight thousand trees have been planted on the peninsula; a new pier has been built; and a river beach has provided new habitats for wildlife. In the long term, that landscape will grow up and flourish, ultimately obliterating the dereliction of an industrial past.

> *What's remarkable about the scale of the Dome is the way you can see it clearly from all sorts of strange places. From the north bank of the Thames it looks so close you wouldn't believe there was a river in between.*
>
> **Richard Rogers, Richard Rogers Partnership**

For the next generation, much less the next one in forty, the figures will ultimately mean nothing. What will remain is the unquantifiable, the legacy you cannot price. At the end of a century of revolutionary change, the Dome has shown that technological developments need not be resisted and feared but have the potential to return us full circle to the natural world. It is computer analysis, specifically computational fluid dynamics, which makes the Dome's lightweight minimal use of materials possible. It is its vast roof, achieved by such means, which allows water to be effectively recycled using the age-old technique of reed-bed filtration.

The Dome, however, has not been created by computers, it has been made by people, many different sorts of people: architects and engineers, designers and artists, performers and abseilers, managers and builders, sponsors and academics, administrators, planners and producers. By anyone's reckoning it ought to have been a cultural collision course from day one, yet the process has demonstrably worked. The creative product of equal competing energies, the Dome has been about new ways of doing things. 'It is extraordinary to think that such a huge team of people has been conjured up out of back rooms all around the country to put this thing together,' says Mark Fisher. 'There have been incredible clashes of culture, but people have reached a long way across their natural borders to communicate with each other.'

Many of those who worked on the Dome remember the Festival of Britain, a national event marked by equally ferocious controversy. No one now recalls what the Festival of Britain cost but plenty of people remember what it meant. Ken Robinson, who lived in Clapham as a child, went to the Festival of Britain and remembered 'what it did for the nation'. Mike Davies was similarly inspired: 'I came to the Festival of Britain when I was nine years old. I stood in front of the Dome of Discovery, the Skylon, I went down the river on the riverbus to Battersea Fun Fair. I remember thinking, "Wow! Is this what architects do?" I never forgot it, it was an inspiration. I hope this exhibition will be the same for young people now.'

Its legacy, the Dome's true meaning, will only be known long after the moment has passed, when the children who are its visitors today grow up and look back. Legacy, in the end, is not a price tag. It's a question. What will we make next? Where will we go? Who will we be?

I think people might make a new species in the future. I'd like there to be chocolate trees.

I'd like things to be more exciting. I'd like more games in school.

People should invest more money in astronomy. I'd like everyone to be vegetarian and more people should be encouraged to use bicycles.

I'd like people to be able to communicate without speaking or making any sounds, just with their thoughts.

I think there will be cars that fly. I'd like robots in my house.

I want every single person in the world to be famous.

Annie, Chris, Louise, Alistair, Jonathan, Vicky, aged 10

| June 1997 | July 1997 | July 1997 | August 1997 | August 1997 |

Chronology

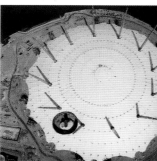

| April 1998 | May 1998 | May 1998 | June 1998 | August 1998 |

October 1997

November 1997

February 1998

March 1998

March 1998

August 1997
Initial responses received for design of the Dome's contents and 22 companies invited to tender; roof fabric contract awarded to Birdair

October 1997
Piling works completed, with 8,000 piles driven in 13 weeks; all 12 masts erected in two weeks; work begins on cable net structure; transport strategy provides for vast majority of visitors to arrive by public transport

December 1997
Eleven exhibit designers announced; discussions begin with Mark Fisher and Peter Gabriel about the creation of the Millennium Show

January 1998
Construction begins on the Dome's inner core service buildings

February 1998
Official launch of proposals for six of the Dome's exhibit zones; draft environmental plan submitted to Greenwich Council

March 1998
Completion of cable net structure; installation of the roof fabric begins

June 1998
Under the National Programme, Children's Promise and Voices of Promise launched; 12 months after start of Dome's construction, the Prime Minister leads celebrations to mark the completion of roof covering at its topping out ceremony; fit-out of core buildings begins

July 1998
Grey water recycling scheme announced, supported by Thames Water; environmental plan accepted by Greenwich Council

September 1998
Training programme begins at Circus Space for the first intake of performers for the Millennium Show

November 1998
400 days to go: confirmed sponsorship stands at £120 million; heavy installation works for the Dome's exhibit zones begins

December 1998
Details of the Faith zone announced; construction of new millennium pier begins

February 1999
Dome structure completed; construction of Skyscape begins; first river boat launched to provide service from Greenwich to the millennium pier at the Dome

March 1999
300 days to go: confirmed sponsorship reaches £142 million; government launches competition to find viable, sustainable future use for the Dome after the completion of the Millennium Experience

June 1999
200 days to go: confirmation that sponsorship reaches and exceeds the target of £150 million

September 1999
100 days to go: final unveiling of the Dome's content; tickets go on sale; phased handover of zones to exhibitors completed

December 1999
Opening celebrations

September 1998

November 1998

January 1999

March 1999

May 1999

Index

Picture credits

The publisher would like to thank the following photographers and organizations for their kind permission to reproduce the images in this book.

NMEC licensed images

© Barry Lewis/Network Photographers: 60 (top right); 60 (bottom left); 60 (bottom right); 61 (all); Buro Happold: 39; 41; © Buro Happold/Mandy Reynolds ABIPP: 8; 31; 50 (bottom); 58; 59; 62 (bottom); 68 (bottom); 69 (top); 69 (bottom); 79; 80 (all); 85 (top); 85 (bottom left); 91 (left); 92 (left); 93 (centre right); 96–7 (all); 101 (all); 111 (bottom right); 112 (bottom right); 127 (top right); 127 (bottom right); 133 (right); 134 (top); 134–5 (bottom); 135 (top left); 135 (top right); 136–7 (all); 139 (all); 140 (centre); 140 (bottom); 142; 177 (right); © Buro Happold/Niels Cross: 135 (bottom right); Dan Pearson: 147; © Gideon Mendel/Network Photographers: 122 (top left); 122 (centre left); 122 (bottom left); 170 (left); 170 (right); 180 (top left); 180 (bottom left); © Jillian Edelstein/Network Photographers: 159 (left); 159 (right); © Jim Byrne/QA Photos: 4–5; 10 (bottom); 36; 48–9 (left); 49 (right); 50 (centre); 64–5; 66–7 (all); 68 (top); 70–1 (all); 72–3 (all); 75; 76–7; 78 (top); 78 (bottom); 81 (all); 82 (right); 82 (bottom); 83; 84; 85 (right); 86 (all); 88; 89; 91 (right); 92 (right); 93 (top); 93 (bottom); 94; 95; 102–3 (all); 104; 105; 107 (top); 107 (bottom); 111 (left); 112 (top left); 112 (top right); 113; 114 (top left); 114 (top right); 115 (top); 115 (bottom); 116–17 (all); 118 (top left); 123 (top right); 123 (bottom left); 124–5 (all); 132–3 (left); 140 (top); 149 (top); 151 (top); 151 (bottom); 152–3 (all); 160; 161 (left); 168–9; 171 (all); 173 (top); 173 (right); 177 (top); 178–9; 181; 184–5; © John Sturrock/Network Photographers: 148 (top); © Jonathan Olley/Network Photographers: 55 (top left); 55 (top right); 55 (centre right); 55 (bottom left); 55 (bottom right); © Justin Leighton/Network Photographers: 55 (centre left); 165 (right); 165 (bottom left); © Mark Power/Network Photographers: 1; 19; 50–1 (top); 53; 56 (left); 56 (right); 60 (top left); 62 (top); 98–9; 108–9; 119; 126–7 (left); 128; 129; 130 (above left); 130 (bottom left); 130 (bottom right); 131; 138; 141; 145; 146; 149 (centre); 149 (right); 156–7 (top); 157 (bottom); 166–7 (left); 167 (right); 174; 175; 177 (bottom left); © Mike Abrahams/Network Photographers: 122 (top right); 122 (centre right); 122 (bottom right); 123 (top right); 123 (bottom right); NMEC: 162 (bottom); Richard Rogers Partnership: 33; 34–5; 161 (right); 165 (top left)

Other images

Aerofilms: 26 (top left); 26 (top right); Chorley Handford: 16–17 (left); 17 (right); 21; 26 (bottom); Claude Nuridsany & Marie Perennou/Science Photo Library: 37; CNES, 1998 distribution SPOT image/Science Photo Library: 10 (top); Dennis Gilbert/View: 118 (top right); London Aerial Photo Library: 106; Martin Jones/Arcaid: 30; 100; Mary Evans Picture Library: 12 (left); 12 (right); © National Maritime Museum London: 23 (left); 23 (right); 24 (bottom); NRSC Ltd/Science Photo Library: 10 (centre); PA/Andrew Stuart: 112 (bottom left); PA/Ben Curtis: 6; 45; 82 (top left); 162 (top); PA/David Giles: 54; PA/Peter Wilcock: 52; PA/Toby Melville: 24 (top); RIBA Library Photography Collection: 13 (all); 15 (left); Richard Rogers Partnership: 28; 29; Richard Waite/Arcaid: 2; 148 (bottom); Sofia Ruiz Bartolini: 15 (right); 87; 114 (bottom left–right); 118 (bottom); 120–1; 130 (top); 143; 154–5 (left); 155 (right); 182; 187; 192; © Steve Bell Associates: 43

Author's dedication

To my children, Katharine and Tom

This edition produced for The Book
People Ltd, Hall Wood Avenue,
Haydock, St Helens, WA11 9UL

First published in 1999 by
HarperCollins*Illustrated*,
an imprint of
HarperCollins*Publishers*
77–85 Fulham Palace Road
London W6 8JB

The HarperCollins website address is:
www.**fire**and**water**.com

NMEC logo © NMEC 1998
and NMEC licensed materials and
illustrations © various agencies

Text © 1999 Elizabeth Wilhide

Elizabeth Wilhide hereby asserts her
moral right to be identified as the
author of this Work.

A CIP catalogue record for this book
is available from the British Library

ISBN: 0 583 34695 2

03 02 01 00 99
9 8 7 6 5 4 3 2 1

Printed and bound in Great Britain
by Bath Press Colourbooks

Author's acknowledgements

In writing this book, I have shared something of the hectic deadline of the Dome. For this reason, I am all the more grateful that very, very busy people have given their time to explain its many complexities to me, to show me slides and drawings, walk me round the site, answer my questions, return my phone calls and read my text. First, I must thank Alex Madina of NMEC, who pointed me in the right direction with immense efficiency, smoothed access to all the different parties and performed the difficult task of collating responses to the first draft.

I must also thank my interviewees, who found spaces in exceptionally tight schedules to talk about a project they were still in the process of creating: Mike Davies and Richard Rogers from Richard Rogers Partnership; Ian Liddell, Glyn Trippick, Paul Westbury, Tony McLaughlin, Peter Scott, Martin Kealey and Helen Elias from Buro Happold; Bernard Ainsworth from the Joint Venture; Gregor Harvie, Sarah Straight, Peter English, David Trench, Dick Coffey, Claire Sampson and Ken Robinson from NMEC; Peter Higgins of Land Design Studio; Mark Fisher; and Dan Pearson. Ian Brack from the Millennium Commission made useful suggestions. Most importantly, I must thank Jennie Page, chief executive of NMEC, for placing the project concisely in context.

At HarperCollins, Clare Baggaley has done a superb job organizing the visual story alongside the text. Richard Atkinson, my editor, read drafts and redrafts with great perception, acted as a crucial sounding board for an evolving structure, and is in no small measure responsible for the merits of the final book. Adam Nicolson provided welcome support. Thanks are also due to Steve Lancashire, headteacher of Canonbury Primary School, Islington, to Tom Mitchell, class teacher, and to the Canonbury parents who gave permission for their children to be interviewed.

Lastly, I must thank family and friends for their forebearance at a time when my working schedule invaded the rest of my life: to Irene Martin and Jim Hardy, Annie and Greg Dinner for taking up the slack; to Glenn and Carol Wilhide; to Ronald Lazenby for test-driving the text, and, most especially, to Martin, Katharine and Tom Lazenby for on-the-spot technical advice, patience and understanding.

Publisher's acknowledgements

The publisher would like to thank Tanya Devonshire-Jones, Kathie Gill, Antonia Maxwell, Barbara Roby and David Stevens for their help with this book.